I CORINTHIANS

William MacDonald

Original text material by William MacDonald
Developed by Emmaus Correspondence School
founded in 1942

ISBN 0-940293-10-2

101112/4321

Front cover: Ruins of Temple of Apollo in Corinth

Printed in the United States of America

OUTLINE OF 1 CORINTHIANS

Lesson 1

Divisions in the Church (1:1—2:16)

INTRODUCTION

The city of Corinth was located in the southern part of Greece, west of Athens. Strategically situated on the trade routes of that day, it became a great center for international commerce, and immense quantities of traffic came to this city. But because of the depraved religion of the people, it soon became the center also for the grossest forms of sin and immorality, so that the name Corinth was a by-word for all that was impure and sensual.

The Apostle Paul first visited Corinth on his second missionary journey. A record of this visit is found in Acts 18. At first he labored among the Jewish people, together with Priscilla and Aquila, his fellow tentmakers. When the Jews rejected the message, he turned to the Gentile people in Corinth. Souls were saved through the preaching of the gospel, and an assembly was formed.

About three years later, when Paul was preaching in Ephesus, he received a letter from Corinth, telling of serious difficulties in the assembly there and also asking various questions as to matters of Christian practice. It was in answer to this letter that the First Epistle to the Corinthians was written.

OUTLINE

  I. Salutation (1:1-3).
 II. Thanksgiving (1:4-9).
    A. For gifts given in the past (vv. 4-6).

1

B. For present fulness of gifts (v. 7).

C. For future preservation of the saints (vv. 8, 9).

III. Divisions in the church (1:10—4:21).

    A. Exhortation to unity (v. 10).

    B. Source of information concerning divisions (v. 11).

    C. Nature of the divisions (v. 12).

    D. Divisions rebuked (vv. 13-17).

      1. Christ is not divided (v. 13).

      2. Only Christ was crucified for them (v. 13).

      3. Believers are baptized unto Christ's Name alone (vv. 13-17).

    E. The folly of exalting men shown by the true nature of the gospel (1:18—3:4).

      1. The message of the cross is the opposite of all that men consider to be true wisdom (vv. 18-25).

      2. The ones whom God calls by the gospel are not generally the ones whom the world considers great (vv. 26-29).

      3. The gospel message exalts God alone and not man (vv. 30, 31).

      4. Paul's example at Corinth was calculated to glorify God and not himself (2:1-5).

      5. Although the gospel does not appeal to human wisdom, yet to those who are mature, it is divine wisdom (2:6—3:4).

        a. It is divine in its origin (vv. 6, 7).

        b. The wisdom has been hidden by God before the world (v. 7).

        c. It was unknown to the rulers of Christ's day (v. 8).

        d. It was revealed to the apostles by the Holy Spirit (vv. 9-12).

        e. It was given by the apostles to others through the inspiration of the Holy Spirit (v. 13).

        f. It can only be understood by those who are enlightened by the Holy Spirit (vv. 14-16).

In the first three verses of this chapter, we have Paul's salutation to the church at Corinth. Verses 4-9 contain Paul's thanksgiving for these believers whom he had led to the Lord. Then in verse 10 he introduces the subject of divisions in the church, a subject which is continued to the end of chapter 4.

GREETINGS FROM PAUL (1:1-3)

Paul was called to be an apostle of Jesus Christ on the Damascus **1:1** road. This call did not come from men, or through men, but directly from the Lord Jesus Christ. An apostle is literally "a sent one." The first apostles were witnesses of Christ in resurrection. They also had the ability to perform miracles as a confirmation that the message they preached was divine. Paul could truly say in the language of Ter Steegen:

> "Christ the Son of God hath sent me to the midnight lands;
> Mine the mighty ordination of the pierced hands."

At the time Paul wrote, a brother named Sosthenes was with him, and so Paul includes his name in the salutation. It cannot be known with certainty whether this is the same Sosthenes we read about in Acts 18:17, the chief ruler of the synagogue who was publicly beaten by the Greeks. There is at least the possibility that this chief ruler had been saved through the preaching of the Apostle and was now helping him in the work of the gospel.

The letter is addressed first of all to the church of God which is at Corinth. It is encouraging to remind our hearts at this point that there is no place on earth too immoral for an assembly belonging to God to be established.

The assembly in Corinth is further described as those that are **1:2** *"sanctified in Christ Jesus, called . . . saints." Sanctified* here means set apart to God from the world, and describes the *position* of all who belong to Christ. As to their *practical condition,* they should set themselves apart day by day in holy living.

There are some who contend that sanctification is a distinct work of grace whereby a person obtains the eradication of the sin nature. Such a teaching is contradicted in this verse. The Corinthian Christians were far from what they should have been in practical holiness, but the fact remains that they were positionally sanctified by God.

As saints they were members of a great fellowship: *"called to be saints, with all that in every place call upon the name of Jesus Christ our*

3

Lord, both theirs and ours." Although the teachings of this epistle were addressed primarily to the saints in Corinth, they are also intended for all those of the world-wide fellowship who acknowledge the Lordship of Christ.

1:3   This epistle is in a very special way the epistle of His Lordship. In discussing the many problems of assembly and personal life, the Apostle constantly reminds his readers that Jesus Christ is Lord and that all we do should be done in acknowledgment of this great truth.

Paul's characteristic greeting is given in verse 3. Grace and peace summarize his entire gospel. Grace is the source of every blessing, and peace is the result in the life of a man who accepts the grace of God. Notice that these great blessings come from God our Father and from the Lord Jesus Christ. Paul does not hesitate to mention the Lord Jesus in the same breath with God the Father. This is one of hundreds of similar expressions in the New Testament implying the equality of the Lord Jesus with God the Father.

PAUL'S THANKSGIVING (1:4-9)

1:4   Having concluded his salutation, the Apostle Paul now turns to thanksgiving for the Corinthians and for the wonderful work of God in their lives (vv. 4-9).

It was a noble trait in the life of the Apostle that always sought to find something thankworthy in the lives of his fellow believers. If their own lives were not very commendable, then he would at least give thanks for what God had done for them. This is exactly the case here. The Corinthians were not what we would call spiritual Christians. But Paul can at least give thanks for the grace of God which was given to them in Christ Jesus.

1:5   The particular way in which God's grace was manifested to the Corinthians was in their being richly endowed with gifts of the Holy Spirit. Paul specifies gifts of utterance and knowledge, presumably meaning that the Corinthians had been given the gifts of tongues, interpretation of tongues, and knowledge to an extraordinary degree. A. T. Robertson points out that utterance has to do with outward expression and knowledge with inward comprehension.

1:6   The fact that they had these gifts was a confirmation of God's work in their lives, and that is what the Apostle Paul means when he says, *"Even as the testimony of Christ was confirmed in you."* They heard the

4

testimony of Christ, they received it by faith, and God testified to the fact that they were truly saved by giving them these miraculous powers.

As far as the possession of gifts was concerned, the Corinthian assembly was not inferior to any other church. But it should be noticed here that the possession of these gifts was not in itself a mark of true spirituality. Paul was really thanking the Lord for something for which the Corinthians themselves were not directly responsible. Gifts are given by the ascended Lord without regard to a person's own merit. If a person has some gift, he should not be proud of it but use it humbly for the Lord. 1:7

The fruit of the Spirit is another matter entirely. This involves the believer's own surrender to the control of the Holy Spirit. The Apostle could not commend the Corinthians for evidence of the fruit of the Spirit in their lives, but only for that which the Lord had sovereignly bestowed on them—something over which they had no control.

Later in the epistle the Apostle will have to reprove the saints for their abuse of these gifts, but here he is content to express thanks that they had received these gifts in such unusual measure.

The Corinthians were waiting for the revelation of our Lord Jesus Christ. Bible students are not agreed as to whether this refers to Christ's coming for His saints (1 Thess. 4:13-18), or the Lord's coming with His saints (2 Thess. 1:6-10). In the first case it would be a revelation of Christ only to believers, whereas in the second it would be His revelation to the whole world. Both the rapture and the glorious appearing of Christ are eagerly awaited by the believer.

Now Paul expresses the further confidence that the Lord will preserve the saints unto the end, that they might be unreprovable in the day of our Lord Jesus Christ. Once again it is striking that Paul's thanksgiving is concerned with what God will do rather than with what the Corinthians have done. Because they have trusted Christ, and because God confirmed this fact by giving the gifts of the Spirit to them, Paul was confident that God would keep them for Himself until Christ's coming for His people. 1:8

Paul's optimism concerning the Corinthians is based upon the faithfulness of God Who called them into the fellowship of His Son. He knows that since God had gone to such tremendous cost to make them sharers of the life of the Lord Jesus, He would never let them 1:9

slip out of His hands.

REBUKE FOR DIVISIONS (1:10-17)

1:10 The Apostle is now ready to take up the problem of divisions in the church (1:10—4:21). He begins with a loving exhortation to unity. Instead of commanding with the authority of an apostle, he beseeches with the tenderness of a brother. The appeal for unity is based on the Name of the Lord Jesus Christ, and since the name stands for the person, it is based on all that the Lord Jesus is and has done. The Corinthians were exalting the name of men; that could only lead to divisions. Paul will exalt the Name of the Lord Jesus, knowing that only in this way will unity be produced among the people of God. *"To speak the same thing"* means to be of one mind and of one accord. It means to be united as to loyalty and allegiance. This unity is produced when Christians have the mind of Christ, and in the verses to follow the Apostle Paul will tell them in a practical manner how they can think Christ's thoughts after Him.

1:11 News concerning the divisions in Corinth had come to Paul from the house of Chloe. In naming his informers, Paul lays down an important principle of Christian conduct. We should not pass on news about our fellow believers unless we are willing to be quoted in the matter. If this example were followed today, it would prevent most of the idle gossip which now plagues the Church.

1:12 Sects or parties were being formed within the local church, each one claiming its distinctive leader. Some acknowledged preference for Paul, some for Apollos, some for Cephas or Peter, and some claimed to belong to Christ, probably meaning that they *alone* belonged to Him, to the exclusion of others.

1:13 Paul's indignant rebuke of sectarianism is found in verses 13-17. To form such parties in the church was to deny the unity of the body of Christ. To follow human leaders was to slight the One Who had been crucified for them. To take the name of a man was to forget that in baptism, they had acknowledged their allegiance to the Lord Jesus.

1:14 The rise of parties in Corinth made Paul thankful that he had baptized only a few in the assembly there. He mentions Crispus and
1:15 Gaius as among those whom he had baptized. He would never want anyone to say that he had baptized in his own name. In other words, he was not trying to win converts to himself or to make a name for

6

himself. His sole aim was to point men and women to the Lord Jesus Christ. On further reflection Paul remembered that he had also bap- **1:16** tized the household of Stephanas, but he could not think of any others.

He explains that Christ did not send him primarily to baptize, but **1:17** to preach the gospel. This does not mean for a moment that Paul did not believe in baptism. He has already mentioned the names of some whom he did baptize. Rather, it means that his main business was not to baptize; he probably entrusted this work to others, perhaps to some of the Christians in the local church. This verse, however, does lend its testimony against any idea that baptism is essential to salvation. If that were true, then Paul would be saying here that he was thankful that he saved none of them save Crispus and Gaius. Such an idea is untenable.

In the latter part of verse 17, we find Paul making an easy transition to the verses that follow. He did not preach the gospel with wisdom of words, lest the cross of Christ should be made of no effect. He knew that if men were impressed by his oratory or rhetoric, then to that extent he had defeated himself in his efforts to set forth the true meaning of the cross of Christ.

It will help us to understand the section that follows if we remember that the Corinthians, being Greeks, were great lovers of human wisdom. They regarded their philosophers as national heroes.

Some of this spirit had apparently crept into the assembly at Corinth. There were those who desired to make the gospel more acceptable to the intelligentsia. They did not feel that it had status among scholars, and so they wanted to intellectualize the message. This worship of intellectualism was apparently one of the issues that was causing the people to form parties around human leaders.

Effort to make the gospel more acceptable are completely misguided. There is a vast difference between God's wisdom and man's, and there is no use trying to reconcile them.

THE CROSS VS. MAN'S WISDOM (1:18-25)

Paul now shows the folly of exalting men, and emphasizes that to do this is inconsistent with the true nature of the gospel (1:18—3:4). His first point is that the message of the cross is the opposite of all that men consider to be true wisdom (1:18-25).

1:18 The message of the cross is foolishness to those who are perishing. As Barnes has so aptly stated, "The death on the cross was associated with the idea of all that is shameful and dishonorable; and to speak of salvation only by the sufferings and death of a crucified man was fitted to excite in their bosoms only unmingled scorn." The Greeks were lovers of wisdom (that is the literal meaning of the word "philosophers"). But there was nothing in the gospel message to appeal to their pride of knowledge.

To those who are saved, the gospel is the power of God. They hear the message, they accept it by faith and the miracle of regeneration is wrought in their lives. Notice the solemn fact in this verse that there are only two classes of people, those who perish and those who are saved. There is no in-between class. Men may love their human wisdom but only the gospel leads to salvation.

1:19 The fact that the gospel would be offensive to human wisdom was prophesied by Isaiah (29:14). There God is quoted as saying, "I will destroy the wisdom of the wise, and will bring to nothing the understanding of the prudent." "The words are God's denouncement of the policy of the 'wise' in Judah in seeking an alliance with Egypt when threatened by Sennacherib"—S. Lewis Johnson in The Wycliffe Bible Commentary. How true it is that God delights to accomplish His purposes in ways that seem foolish to men. How often He uses methods that the wise of this world would ridicule, yet they achieve the desired results with wonderful accuracy and efficiency. For example, man's wisdom assures him that he can earn or merit his own salvation. The gospel sets aside all man's efforts to save himself and presents Christ as the only way to God.

1:20 Paul next hurls out a defiant challenge. Where is the wise? Where is the scribe? Where is the disputer of this world? Did God consult them when He devised His plan of salvation? Could they ever have worked out such a scheme of redemption if left to their own wisdom? Can they rise to disprove anything that God has ever said? The answer is an emphatic "No." God has made foolish the wisdom of this world.

1:21 Man cannot by his own wisdom come to the knowledge of God. For centuries God gave the human race this opportunity, and the result was failure. Then it pleased God by the preaching of the cross, a message that seems foolish to men, to save those who believe. The thought here is not so much the foolishness of preaching as the

8

foolishness of the thing preached, that is, the Cross. Of course, we know that it is not foolishness, but it seems foolish to the unenlightened mind of man. Godet says that this sentence (v. 21) contains a whole philosophy of history, the substance of entire volumes. The student should not hurry over it quickly, but ponder deeply its tremendous truths.

It was characteristic of the Jewish people to seek for a sign. Their **1:22** attitude was that they would believe if some miracle were shown to them. The Greeks on the other hand loved wisdom. They were interested in human reasonings, in arguments, in logic. But Paul did **1:23** not cater to their desires. He says, "We preach Christ crucified." As someone has said, "He was not a sign-loving Jew, nor a wisdom-loving Greek, but a Savior-loving Christian."

To the Jews, Christ crucified was a stumbling block. They looked for a mighty military leader to deliver them from the oppression of Rome. Instead of this, the gospel offered them a Savior Who was nailed to a cross of shame. To the Gentiles, Christ crucified was foolishness. They could not understand how One Who died in such seeming weakness and failure could ever solve their problems.

But strangely enough, the very things that the Jews and the Gen- **1:24** tiles sought are found in a wonderful way in the Lord Jesus. To those who hear His call and trust in Him, both Jews and Gentiles, He becomes the power of God and the wisdom of God.

Actually, of course, there is neither foolishness nor weakness with **1:25** God. But the Apostle is saying in verse 25 that what seems to be foolishness on God's part, in the eyes of men, is actually wiser than man at his very best. Also, what seems to be weakness on God's part, in the eyes of men, turns out to be more powerful than anything that man can produce.

THE GOSPEL'S APPEAL (1:26-31)

Having spoken of the gospel itself, the Apostle now turns to the **1:26** people whom God calls by the gospel (vv. 26-29). He reminds the Corinthians that not many wise after the flesh, not many mighty, not many noble are called. It has often been pointed out that the text does not say "not any" but "not many." Because of this slight difference, one titled English lady used to testify that she was saved by the letter "m."

9

The Corinthians themselves had not come from the upper intellectual crust of society. They had not been reached by high-sounding philosophies but by the simple gospel. Why, then, were they putting such a premium on human wisdom and exalting preachers who sought to make the message palatable to the worldly-wise?

If men were to build a church they would seek to enroll the most prominent members of the community. But verse 26 teaches us that what men esteem so highly, God passes by. The ones whom He calls are not generally the ones whom the world considers great.

1:27 God chose the foolish things of the world that He might put to shame them that are wise; and the weak things of the world that He might put to shame the things that are strong. "The more primitive the material, the greater—if the same high standard of art can be reached—the honor of the Master; the smaller the army, the mightier—if the same great victory can be won—the praise of the conqueror"—Sauer.

God used trumpets to bring down the walls of Jericho. He reduced Gideon's army from 32,000 to 300 to rout the hosts of Midian. He used an oxgoad in the hand of Shamgar to defeat 600 Philistines. With the jawbone of an ass, He enabled Samson to defeat a whole army. And our Lord fed over 5,000 with nothing more than a few loaves and fishes.

1:28 To make up what someone has called "God's five-ranked army of fools," Paul adds the base things of the world, the things that are despised and the things that are not. Using such unlikely materials, God brings to nought the things that are. In other words, He loves to take up people who are of no esteem in the eyes of the world and use them to glorify Himself. These verses should serve as a rebuke to Christians who curry the favor of prominent and well-known personages and show little or no regard for the more humble saints of God.

1:29 God's purpose in choosing those of no account in the eyes of the world is that all the glory should accrue to Himself and not to man. Since salvation is entirely of Him, He alone is worthy to be praised.

1:30 Verse 30 emphasizes even further that all we are and have comes from Him, not from philosophy, and that there is therefore no room for human glory. The verse might be paraphrased as follows: "But by Him (God) are ye placed in Christ Jesus, who was made unto us wisdom from God, and righteousness, and sanctification, and redemption."

10

First of all, Christ is made unto us wisdom. He is the wisdom of God (v. 24), the One whom God's wisdom chose as the way of salvation. When we have Him, we have a positional wisdom that guarantees our full salvation. Secondly, He is our righteousness. Through faith in Him we are reckoned righteous by a holy God. Thirdly, He is our sanctification. In ourselves we have nothing in the way of personal holiness, but in Him we are positionally sanctified, and by His power we are transformed from one degree of sanctification to another. Finally, He is our redemption, and this doubtless speaks of redemption in its final aspect when the Lord will come and take us home to be with Himself, and when we shall be redeemed— spirit, soul and body.

"Wisdom out of Christ is damning folly—righteousness out of Christ is guilt and condemnation—sanctification out of Christ is filth and sin—redemption out of Christ is bondage and slavery"—Traill.

A. T. Pierson relates verse 30 to the life and ministry of our Lord. "His deeds and His words and His practices, these show Him as the wisdom of God. Then come His death, burial, and resurrection: these have to do with our righteousness. Then His forty days' walk among men, His ascension up on high, the gift of the Spirit, and His session at the right hand of God, have to do with our sanctification. Then His coming again, which has to do with our redemption."

Some see verse 30 as an outline of the entire epistle, as follows:

Wisdom	Chapters 1-4
Righteousness	Chapters 5-10
Sanctification	Chapters 11-14
Redemption	Chapter 15
Postscript	Chapter 16

1:31 God has so arranged it that all these blessings should come to us in the Lord Jesus Christ. Paul's argument therefore is, "Why glory in men? They cannot do any one of these things for you."

PAUL'S EXAMPLE AT CORINTH (2:1-5)

2:1 The Apostle now reminds the saints of his ministry among them and how he sought to glorify God and not himself. He came to them proclaiming the testimony of God, not with excellency of speech or of wisdom. He was not at all interested in showing himself off as an orator or as a philosopher.

11

This shows that the Apostle Paul recognized the difference between ministry that is soulish and that which is spiritual. By soulish ministry, we mean that which amuses, entertains, or generally appeals to man's emotions. Spiritual ministry, on the other hand, presents the truth of God's Word in such a way as to reach the heart and conscience of the hearers.

2:2 The content of Paul's message was Jesus Christ and Him crucified. "Jesus Christ" refers to His Person, while "Him crucified" refers to His work. The Person and work of the Lord Jesus form the substance of the Christian evangel.

2:3 Paul further emphasizes that his personal demeanor was neither impressive nor attractive. He was with the Corinthians in weakness and in fear and in much trembling. The treasure of the gospel was contained in an earthen vessel that the excellency of the power might be of God and not of Paul. He himself was an example of how God

2:4 uses weak things to confound the mighty. Neither Paul's speech nor his preaching were in persuasive words of wisdom, but in demonstration of the Spirit and of power. Some suggest that his speech refers to the material he presented and his preaching to the manner of its presentation. Others define his speech as his witness to individuals and his preaching as his messages to groups. According to the standards of this world, the Apostle might never have won an oratorical contest. Notwithstanding this, the Spirit of God used the message to produce conviction of sin and conversion to God.

2:5 Paul knew that there was the utmost danger that his hearers might be interested in himself or in his own personality rather than in the living Lord. Conscious of his own inability to bless or to save, he determined that he would lead men to trust in God alone rather than in the wisdom of men. It is fitting that all who proclaim the gospel message or teach the Word of God should make this their constant aim.

THE NATURE OF THE GOSPEL (2:6-16)

2:6 First of all, wisdom shown in the gospel is divine in its origin (vv. 6, 7). *"We speak wisdom among them that are perfect,"* that is, among those Christians who are full-grown or mature. Yet it is not wisdom as the world reckons it, nor would it be wisdom in the eyes of the princes or rulers of this world. Their wisdom is a perishable thing which, like themselves, is born for one brief day.

We speak God's wisdom in a mystery. A mystery is a New Testa- **2:7** ment truth not hitherto revealed, but now made known to believers by the apostles and prophets of the early Church age. This mystery is a wisdom that has been hidden, which God foreordained before the worlds unto our glory. The mystery of the gospel includes such wonderful truths as the fact that now Jews and Gentiles are made one in Christ; that the Lord Jesus will come and take His waiting people home to be with Himself; and that not all believers will die but all will be changed.

The rulers of this age may refer to demonic spirit beings in the **2:8** heavenlies or to their human agents on earth. They didn't understand the hidden wisdom of God (Christ on a cross) or realize that their murder of the Holy Son of God would result in their own destruction. If they had known the ways of God they would not have crucified the Lord of glory.

The process of revelation, inspiration, and illumination are de- **2:9** scribed in verses 9-16. They tell us how these wonderful truths were made known to the apostles by the Holy Spirit, how they, in turn, passed on these truths to us by inspiration of the Holy Spirit, and how we understand them by the illumination of the Holy Spirit.

1. Revelation (2:9-12)

The quotation in verse 9 from Isaiah 64:4 is a prophecy that God had treasured up wonderful truths which could not be discovered by the natural senses but which in due time He would reveal to those who loved Him. Three faculties (eye, ear and heart or mind) by which we learn earthly things are listed, but these are not sufficient for the reception of divine truths, for there the Spirit of God is necessary.

This verse is commonly interpreted to refer to the glories of heaven, and once we get that meaning in our minds, it is difficult to dislodge it and accept any other meaning. But Paul is really speaking here about the truths that have been revealed for the first time in the New Testament. Men could never have arrived at these truths through scientific investigations or philosophic inquiries. The human mind, left to itself, could never discover the wonderful mysteries which were made known at the beginning of the gospel era. Human reason is totally inadequate to find the truth of God.

2:10 That verse 9 does not refer to heaven is proved by the statement that "God has revealed them unto us by His Spirit." In other words, these truths foretold in the Old Testament were made known to the apostles of the New Testament era. The "us" refers to the writers of the New Testament. It was by the Spirit of God that the apostles and prophets were enlightened, because the Spirit searches all things, yea, the deep things of God. In other words, the Spirit of God, one of the members of the Godhead, is infinite in wisdom and understands all the truths of God and is able to impart them to others.

2:11 Even in human affairs no one knows what a man is thinking but he himself. No one else can possibly find out unless the man himself chooses to make it known. Even then, in order to understand a man, a person must have the spirit of a man. An animal could not fully understand our thinking. So it is with God. The only one who can understand the things of God is the Spirit of God.

2:12 The "we" of verse 12 refers to the writers of the New Testament, although it is equally true of all the Bible writers, of course. Since the apostles and prophets had received the Holy Spirit, He was able to share with them the deep truths of God. That is what the Apostle means when he says in this verse, "Now we have received, not the spirit of the world, but the spirit which is of God, that we might know the things that are freely given to us of God." Apart from the Spirit of God, the apostles could never have received the divine truths of which Paul is speaking and which are preserved for us in the New Testament.

2. Inspiration (2:13)

2:13 Having described the process of revelation, by which the writers of Sacred Scripture received truth from God, Paul now goes on to describe the process of inspiration, by which that truth was communicated to us. Verse 13 is one of the strongest passages in the Word of God on the subject of verbal inspiration. The Apostle Paul clearly states that in conveying these truths to us, the apostles did not use words of their own choosing or words dictated by human wisdom. Rather, they used the very words which the Holy Spirit taught them to use. And so we believe that the actual words of Scripture, as found in the original autographs, were the very words of God (and that the Bible in its present form is entirely trustworthy).

14

At this point a howl of objection arises since what we have said implies mechanical dictation, as if God did not allow the writers to use their own style. Yet we know that Paul's writing style is quite different from Luke's, for example. How, then can we reconcile verbal inspiration with the obvious individual style of the writers? In some way which we do not understand, God gave the very words of Scripture, and yet he clothed those words with the individual style of the writers. Remembering that, we should have no trouble with the idea of mechanical dictation. But why should we have trouble anyway? When an executive dictates a letter to his secretary, he wants it transcribed exactly as he gives it. He does not want her to inject her own ideas or expressions. If an executive has that right, should we deny it to God?

The expression "comparing spiritual things with spiritual" can be explained in several ways. It may mean (1) teaching spiritual truths with Spirit-given words; (2) communicating spiritual truths to spiritual men; (3) comparing spiritual truths in one section of the Bible with those in another. We believe that the first explanation is the one that best fits in the context. Paul is saying that the process of inspiration involves the conveying of divine truth with words that are especially chosen for the purpose by the Holy Spirit. Thus the New International Version translates, ". . . expressing spiritual truths in spiritual words."

It is sometimes objected that this passage cannot refer to inspiration because Paul says "we speak," not "we write." But it is not uncommon to find the verb "to speak" used of inspired writings (e.g., John 12:38, 41; Acts 28:25; 2 Peter 1:21).

3. Illumination (2:14-16)

Not only is the gospel divine in its revelation and divine in its inspiration, but now we learn that it can only be received by the power of the Spirit of God. Unaided, the natural man cannot receive the things of the Spirit of God. They are foolishness to him. He cannot possibly understand them because they can only be spiritually understood. **2:14**

"The wise Christian wastes no time trying to explain God's program to unregenerate men; it would be casting pearls before swine. He might as well try to describe a sunset to a blind man or discuss

15

nuclear physics with a monument in a city park. The natural man cannot receive such things. One might as well try to catch sunbeams with a fishhook as to lay hold of God's revelation unassisted by the Holy Spirit. Unless one is born of the Spirit and taught by Him, all this is utterly foreign to him. Being a Ph.D does not help, for in this realm it could mean 'Phenomenal Dud'!!"—Vance Havner.

2:15 On the other hand, the man who is illuminated by the Spirit of God can discern these wonderful truths even though he himself cannot be understood by the unconverted. Perhaps he is a lowly carpenter, or plumber, or fisherman; yet he is an able student of the Holy Scriptures. "The Spirit-controlled Christian investigates, inquires into, and scrutinizes the Bible and comes to an appreciation and understanding of its contents"—Wuest. To the world he is an enigma. He may never have been to a college or a seminary, yet he can understand the deep mysteries of the Word of God and perhaps even teach them to others.

2:16 The Apostle now asks the rhetorical question: "Who has known the mind of the Lord, that he should instruct Him?" (NASB). To ask the question is to answer it. God cannot be known through the wisdom or power of men. He is known only as He chooses to make Himself known. However, those who have the mind of Christ are able to understand the deep truths of God.

First, there is *revelation* (vv. 9-12). This means that God revealed hitherto unknown truths to men by the Holy Spirit. These truths were made known supernaturally by the Spirit of God.

Second, there is *inspiration* (v. 13). In transmitting these truths to others, the apostles (and all other writers of the Bible) used the very words which the Holy Spirit taught them to use.

Finally, there is *illumination* (vv. 14-16). Not only must these truths be miraculously *revealed* and miraculously *inspired*, but they can only be *understood* by the supernatural power of the Holy Spirit.

When you have mastered this lesson, take the first part of Exam 1 (covering lesson 1), questions 1-10 on pages 7-10.

Don't Exalt Men (3:1—4:21)

OUTLINE

III. Divisions in the church (1:10—4:21).
   E. The folly of exalting men shown by the true nature of the gospel (1:18—3:4). (cont'd).
      5. Although the gospel does not appeal to human wisdom, yet to those who are mature, it is divine wisdom (2:6—3:4). (cont'd).
         g. Because of their carnality, Paul had not been able to impart deep truths to the Corinthians (3:1-4).
   F. The folly of exalting men shown by the true nature of the Christian ministry (3:5—4:21).
      1. These men are only servants (3:5).
      2. They cannot produce spiritual life (vv. 6, 7).
      3. In a coming day, their work will be judged and rewarded (v. 8).
      4. God is the One to whom all are responsible (vv. 9-17).
         a. Paul laid the foundation of the church in Corinth (v. 10a) and others have been building on it (v. 10b).
         b. The foundation is Christ (v. 11).
         c. Service in connection with the church may be of three types (vv. 12-17).
            (1) Good worker rewarded (vv. 12-14).
            (2) Worthless worker suffers loss but he is saved (v. 15).
            (3) Destructive worker destroyed (vv. 16, 17).
      5. True wisdom for a servant of Christ is in the knowledge of one's own nothingness (vv, 18-20).

6. Instead of choosing favorite leaders, we should realize that they all belong to us (v. 21), and that ultimately all belong to God (v. 23).
7. Christian leaders are servants and stewards (4:1-5).
    a. Stewards are required to be faithful (vv. 1, 2).
    b. Others cannot judge this. Nor can a person judge his own faithfulness. Only God can do this (vv. 3, 4).
    c. Therefore, judgment should be left to Him (v. 5).
8. Pride is the cause of the divisions (4:6-13).
    a. Paul used himself and Apollos as examples to teach the folly of glorifying human leaders (v. 6).
    b. We have nothing we did not receive (v. 7).
    c. The Corinthians were living as kings ahead of the proper time (v. 8).
    d. The apostles, on the other hand, were living in the poorest of circumstances (vv. 9-13).
9. Final admonition on the subject of divisions (4:14-21).
    a. Paul, as their father in the faith, beseeches them to imitate him (vv. 14-16).
    b. He is sending Timothy to remind them of Paul's example (v. 17).
    c. This does not mean that Paul is not going to Corinth (vv. 18, 19). He will go.
    d. Then he will know whether those who cause divisions have mere words or spiritual power also (vv. 19, 20).
    e. The mood of his coming will depend on the Corinthians themselves (v. 21).

THE CARNALITY OF THE CORINTHIANS (3:1-4)

3:1 When Paul first visited Corinth, he had fed the believers with the elementary milk of the Word because they were weak and young in the faith. The teaching which had been given to them was suitable to their condition. They could not receive deeply spiritual instruction 3:2 because they were new believers. They were mere babes in Christ. Paul had taught them only the elementary truths concerning Christ, which he speaks of as milk. They were not able to take more solid food (meat) because of their immaturity. In the same vein, the Lord

Jesus said to His disciples, "I have yet many things to say unto you, but ye cannot bear them now" (John 16:12).

With regard to the Corinthians, the tragic thing was that they still had not improved sufficiently to receive deeper truth from the Apostle. The believers were in a carnal or fleshly state of soul. This was **3:3** evidenced by the fact that there was jealousy and strife among them. Such behavior is characteristic of the men of this world, but not of those who are led by the Spirit of God.

In forming parties around human leaders, such as Paul and Apol- **3:4** los, they were acting on a purely human level. That is what Paul means when he asks, "Are you not *mere* men?" (NASB).

Up to this point, the Apostle Paul had been showing the folly of exalting men by a consideration of the true nature of the gospel message. He now turns to the subject of the Christian ministry and shows that from this standpoint also, it is sheer foolishness to exalt religious leaders by building parties around them.

MEN ARE ONLY SERVANTS (3:5-8)

Apollos and Paul were servants by whom the Corinthians had come **3:5** to believe in the Lord Jesus. They were simply agents and not the heads of rival schools. How unwise then of the Corinthians to raise servants to the rank of master. Dr. H. A. Ironside quaintly comments at this point, "Imagine a household divided over servants."

Using a figure from agriculture, Paul shows that the servant is after **3:6** all very limited in what he can do. Paul himself could plant and Apollos could water, but only God could give the increase. So today, some of us can preach the Word and all of us can pray for unsaved relatives and friends, but the actual work of salvation can only be done by the Lord. Looking at it from this point, we can readily see **3:7** that the planter and the waterer are really not very important, relatively speaking. They have not the power in themselves to bring forth life. Why then should there be any envy or rivalry among Christian workers? Each should do the work that has been allotted to him, and rejoice when the Lord shows His hand in blessing. He that **3:8** planteth and he that watereth are one in the sense that they both have the same object and aim. There should be no jealousy between them. As far as service is concerned, they are on the same level. In a coming day, each will receive his own reward according to his own labor. That day, of course, refers to the Judgment Seat of Christ.

ALL ARE ACCOUNTABLE TO GOD (3:9-17)

3:9 God is the one to whom all are responsible. All His servants are fellow-workers, laboring together in God's tilled harvest field, or, to change the picture, working together on the same building. The King James Version renders verse 9 as "For we are labourers together with God." This creates the impression that God is working and we are all working together with Him. But the thought might be more accurately rendered as, "We are fellow-workers who belong to God and are working with one another"—Erdman.

3:10 Continuing with the idea of building, the Apostle first of all acknowledges that anything he has been able to accomplish has been due to the grace of God. By this he means the undeserved ability from God to do the work of an apostle. Then he goes on to describe his part in the beginning of this assembly at Corinth. "As a wise masterbuilder, I have laid the foundation." He came to Corinth preaching Christ and Him crucified. Souls were saved and a local church was planted. Then he adds, "And another buildeth thereon." By this, he doubtless refers to other teachers who subsequently visited Corinth and built on the foundation which had already been established there. But the Apostle cautions, "Let each man take heed how he buildeth thereupon." He means that it is a solemn thing to exercise a teaching ministry in the local church. Some had come to Corinth with divisive doctrines and with teachings that were contrary to the Word of God. The Apostle was doubtless conscious of these teachers as he penned the words.

3:11 Only one foundation is required for a building. Once it is laid, it never needs to be repeated. The Apostle Paul had laid the foundation of the church at Corinth. That foundation was Jesus Christ, His Person and Work.

3:12 Subsequent teaching in a local church may be of varying degrees of value. For instance, some teaching is of lasting worth, and might be likened to gold, silver, or precious stones. Here precious stones do not refer to diamonds, rubies, or other gems but rather to the granite, marble, or alabaster which were used in the construction of costly temples. On the other hand, teaching in the local church might be of passing value or of no value at all. Such teaching is likened to wood, hay, and stubble.

The passage of Scripture we are now studying is commonly used in a general way to refer to the lives of all Christian believers. It is true that we are all building, day by day, and the results of our work will be manifested in a coming day. However, a careful student of the Bible will want to note that the passage does not refer primarily to all believers but rather to preachers, teachers, or other Christian workers.

In a coming day, every man's work will be manifest. This day, of **3:13** course, refers to the Judgment Seat of Christ when all service for the Lord will be reviewed. The process of review is likened to the action of fire. Service that has brought glory to God and blessing to man, like gold, silver, and precious stones, will not be affected by the fire. On the other hand, that which has caused trouble among the people of God or failed to edify them will be consumed. "The fire shall try every man's work of what sort it is."

Service in connection with the church may be of three types. In **3:14** verse 14 we have the first type—service that has been of a profitable nature. In such a case, the servant's life work stands the test of the Judgment Seat of Christ and the worker is rewarded.

The second type of service is that which is useless. In this case, the **3:15** servant suffers loss, although he himself is saved, yet as by fire. "Loss does not imply the forfeiture of something once possessed, but rather the failure to obtain what one might have possessed"—E. W. Rogers. It should be clear from this verse that the Judgment Seat of Christ is not concerned in any way with the subject of a believer's sins and their penalty. The penalty of a believer's sins was borne by the Lord Jesus Christ on the Cross of Calvary, and that matter has been settled once and for all. Thus the believer's salvation is not at all in question at the Judgment Seat of Christ; rather it is a matter of his service.

Through failure to understand the distinction between salvation and rewards, some have based their teaching of purgatory on this verse. However, a careful examination of the verse reveals no hint as to purgatory. There is no thought that the fire purifies the character of a man. Rather the fire tests a man's work or service, of what sort it is. The man is saved despite the fact that his works are consumed by the fire.

An interesting thought in connection with this verse is that the

21

Word of God is sometimes likened to fire (see Isa. 5:24 and Jer. 23:29). The same Word of God which will test our service at the Judgment Seat of Christ is available to us now. If we are building in accordance with the teachings of the Bible, then our work will stand the test in that coming day.

3:16　Paul reminds the believers that they are a temple of God and that the Spirit of God dwells in them. It is true that every individual believer is also a temple of God indwelt by the Holy Spirit, but that is not the thought here. The Apostle is looking at the church as a collective company, and wishes them to realize the holy dignity of such a calling.

3:17　A third class of service in the local church is that which may be spoken of as destructive. Apparently there were false teachers who had come into the church at Corinth and whose instruction tended more to sin than to holiness. They did not think it a serious matter to thus cause havoc in a temple of God, so Paul thunders out this solemn declaration, "If any man defile the temple of God, him shall God destroy." Viewed in its local setting, this means that if any man enters a local church and wrecks its testimony, God will destroy him. The passage is speaking of false teachers who are not true believers in the Lord Jesus. The seriousness of such an offense is indicated by the closing words of verse 17, "for the temple of God is holy, which temple ye are."

TRUE WISDOM (3:18-23)

3:18　In Christian service, as in all of Christian life, there is always the danger of self-deception. Perhaps some of those who came to Corinth as teachers posed as men of extreme wisdom. Any who have an exalted view of their own worldly wisdom must learn that they must become fools in the eyes of the world in order to become wise in God's estimation. Godet helpfully paraphrases at this point: "If any individual whatever, Corinthian or other, while preaching the gospel in your assemblies assumes the part of a wise man and reputation of a profound thinker, let him assure himself that he will not attain to true wisdom until he has passed through a crisis in which that wisdom of his with which he is puffed up will perish and after which only he will receive the wisdom which is from above."

3:19　The wisdom of this world is foolishness with God. Man by search-

22

ing could never find out God, neither would human wisdom ever have devised a plan of salvation by which God would become Man in order to die for guilty, vile, rebel sinners. Job 5:13 is quoted in verse 19 to show that God triumphs over the supposed wisdom of men to work out His own purposes. Man with all his learning cannot thwart the plans of the Lord; instead, He often shows them that in spite of their worldly wisdom, they are utterly poor and powerless.

Psalm 94:11 is quoted in verse 20 to emphasize that the Lord **3:20** knows all the reasonings of the wise men of this world, and He further knows that they are vain, empty, and fruitless. But why is Paul going to such pains to discredit worldly wisdom? Simply for this reason—the Corinthians were placing a great premium on such wisdom and were following those leaders who seemed to exhibit it in a remarkable degree.

In view of all that had been said, no one should glory in men. And **3:21** as far as true servants of the Lord are concerned, we should not boast that we belong to them but rather realize that they belong to us. "All things are yours."

Someone has called verse 22 "an inventory of the possessions of **3:22** the child of God." Christian workers belong to us, whether Paul the evangelist, or Apollos the teacher, or Cephas the pastor. Since they all belong to us, it is folly for us to claim that we belong to any one of them. Then the world is ours. As joint heirs with Christ, we will one day come into possession of it, but in the meantime it is ours by divine promise. Those who tend its affairs do not realize that they are doing so for us. Life is ours. By this we do not mean merely existence on earth but life in its truest, fullest sense. And death is ours. For us it is no longer a dread foe that consigns us to the dark unknown; rather, it is now the messenger of God that brings the soul to heaven. Things present and things to come are likewise ours. It has been truly said that all things serve the man who serves Christ. A. T. Robertson once said, "The stars in their courses fight for the man who is partner with God in the world's redemption."

All Christians belong to Christ. Some in Corinth were claiming to **3:23** belong to Him to the exclusion of all others. They formed the "Christ-party." But Paul refutes any such contention. We are all Christ's, and Christ is God's. By thus showing the saints their true and proper dignity, Paul reveals in bold relief the folly of forming parties and divisions in the church.

23

CHRISTIAN LEADERS ARE STEWARDS (4:1-5)

4:1 In order that the saints might have a proper appraisal of Paul and the other apostles, he says that they should look upon them as ministers or assistants of Christ and stewards of the mysteries of God. The word "minister" simply means a servant and never denotes a person in charge of a local church, as it is used today. A steward is a servant who cares for the person or property of another. The mysteries of God were the previously hidden secrets which God revealed to the apostles and prophets of the New Testament period.

4:2 A major requirement in a steward is that he be found faithful. Man values cleverness, wisdom, and wealth; but God is looking for those
4:3 who will be faithful to Jesus in all things. The faithfulness that is required in stewards is a difficult thing for man to evaluate. That is why Paul says here that "With me it is a very small thing that I should be judged of you, or of man's judgment." Paul realizes how utterly unable man is to form a competent judgment of true faithfulness to God. He adds, "Yea, I judge not mine own self." He realized that he was born into the human family with a judgment that was constantly biased in his own favor.

4:4 When the Apostle says, *"I know nothing by myself,"* he means that in the matter of Christian service, he is not conscious of any charge of unfaithfulness that might be brought against him. He does not mean for a moment that he does not know of any sin in his life or any way in which he falls short of perfection. The passage should be read in the light of the context, and the subject here is Christian service and faithfulness in it. But even if he did not know anything against himself, yet he was not thereby justified. He simply was not competent to judge in the matter. After all, the Lord is the judge.

4:5 In view of this, we should be extremely careful in our appraisal of Christian service. We tend to exalt that which is spectacular and sensational, and depreciate that which is menial or inconspicuous. The safe policy is to judge nothing before the time, but to wait until the Lord comes. He will be able to judge, not only what is seen by the eye, but also the motives of the heart: not only what was done, but why it was done. He will make manifest the counsels of the heart, and, needless to say, anything that was done for self-display or self-glory will fail to receive a reward.

When Paul says at the end of this verse, *"then shall every man have praise of God,"* this is not to be taken as a flat promise that every believer's service will show up in a favorable way in that day. The meaning is that every one who deserves praise will receive praise from God and not from men.

PRIDE CAUSES DIVISIONS (4:6-13)

In the next eight verses, the Apostle states quite clearly that pride is **4:6** the cause of the divisions that have come into the church at Corinth.

He first explains, here in verse six, that in speaking about the Christian ministry and the tendency to follow human leaders (Chapters 3:5—4:5), he used himself and Apollos as the examples. In other words, the Corinthians were not forming parties around Paul and Apollos, alone, but also around other men who were then in their church. However, out of a sense of Christian courtesy and delicacy, Paul transferred the entire matter to Apollos and himself so that by their example the saints would learn not to have exaggerated opinions of their leaders or to gratify their pride by the formation of parties. He wanted the saints to evaluate everything and everyone by what is written in the Scriptures.

If one Christian teacher is more gifted than another, it is because **4:7** God made him so. Everything he has, he received from the Lord. In fact it is true of all of us that everything we have has been given to us by God. That being the case, why should we be proud or puffed up? Our talents and gifts are not the result of our own cleverness.

The Corinthians had become self-sufficient; they were filled. They **4:8** prided themselves on the abundance of spiritual gifts in their midst; they were rich. They were living in luxury, comfort, and ease. There was no sense of need. They acted as if they were already reigning, but they were doing so without the apostles. Paul states that he wishes that the time to reign had already come so that he might reign with them. But in the meantime, "lifetime is training time for reigning time," as someone has said. Christians will reign with the Lord Jesus Christ when He comes back and sets up His kingdom on earth. In the meantime, their privilege is to share the reproach of a rejected Savior. "It is positive disloyalty to seek our crown before the King gets his. Yet this is what some of the Christians at Corinth were doing. The apostles themselves were bearing the reproach of Christ. But the Corinthian Christians were 'rich' and 'honorable.' They were

25

seeking a good time where their Lord and Master had such a hard time"—H. P. Barker. It has been pointed out that at official coronations, the peers and peeresses never put on their coronets until the sovereign has been crowned. The Corinthians were reversing this; they were already reigning whereas the Lord was still in rejection.

4:9   In contrast to the self-satisfaction of the Corinthians, Paul describes the lot of the apostles. He pictures them as thrown into the arena with wild beasts while men and angels look on. As Godet has said, "It was no time for the Corinthians to be self-complacent and boasting, while the church was on the throne and the apostles were

4:10   under the sword." While the apostles were treated as fools for Christ's sake, the saints enjoyed prestige in the community as wise Christians. The apostles were weak, but the Corinthians suffered no infirmity. In contrast to the dishonor of the apostles was the glory of

4:11   the saints. It did not seem to the apostles that the hour of triumph or of reigning had come. They were suffering from hunger and thirst and nakedness and persecution. They were hunted, chased and

4:12   pursued, having no certain dwelling place. They supported themselved by working with their own hands. For reviling, they returned blessing. When they were persecuted, they did not fight back, but

4:13   patiently endured. When defamed, they entreated men to accept the Lord Jesus. In short, they were made as the filth of the world, the scum of all things. This description of suffering for the sake of Christ should speak to all our hearts. If the Apostle Paul were living today could he say to us, as he said to the Corinthians, "Ye have come to reign without us"?

FINAL WARNING ABOUT DIVISIONS (4:14-21)

4:14   From verse 14 through verse 21, Paul gives a final admonition to the believers on the subject of divisions. Conscious of the fact that he has been using irony, he explains that he has not done so to shame the Christians, but rather to admonish them as his beloved children. He was not inspired by bitterness to speak as he had done, but rather by a sincere interest in their spiritual welfare.

4:15   The Apostle reminds them that though they might have ten thousand teachers yet they have only one father in the faith. Paul himself had led them to the Lord; he was their spiritual father. Many others might come along to teach them, but no others could have the

26

same tender regard for them as the one who pointed them to the Lamb. Paul does not at all intend to depreciate the ministry of teaching, but is simply stating what we all know to be true, namely, that many can be engaged in Christian service without the personal interest in the saints that is characteristic of one who has pointed them to Christ.

Paul therefore urges them to be imitators of himself, that is, in his **4:16** unselfish devotion to Christ and in his tireless love and service for his fellow believers, such as he has described in verses 9-13. In order to **4:17** help them reach this goal, Paul sent Timothy to them, his beloved and faithful child in the Lord. Timothy was instructed to remind them of Paul's ways in Christ, ways which he taught in all the churches. In verse 17 Paul is saying that he practiced what he preached, and this should be true of everyone who engages in Christian service.

When Paul explained that he was sending Timothy to them, **4:18** perhaps some of his detractors in Corinth would rise quickly to suggest that Paul was afraid to come himself. These men were puffed up, suggesting that Paul would not come personally. But he promises **4:19** that he will come in the near future, if the Lord wills. When he does, he will expose the pride of those who can talk so freely, but have no spiritual power. After all, it is power that counts, for the kingdom of **4:20** God is not concerned principally with words but with action. It does not consist of profession, but of reality. The manner in which Paul **4:21** comes to them will depend on themselves. If they show a rebellious spirit, he will come to them with a rod. If, on the other hand, they are humble and submissive, he will come in love and in the spirit of meekness.

When you are ready, complete Exam 1 by answering questions 11-20 on pages 10-12. (You should have already answered questions 1-10 as part of your study of Lesson 1.)

27

Lesson 3

Moral and Material Wrongs 5:1—6:20

OUTLINE

IV. Discipline in the church (5:1-13).
   A. The need for discipline—a case of incest (v. 1).
   B. The attitude of the church—pride instead of mourning (v. 2).
   C. Paul's judgment in the matter—deliver the offender over to Satan (vv. 3-5).
   D. The danger of delay—sin acts like leaven (vv. 6-8).
      1. It affects all the church (v. 6).
      2. It should be put away (v. 7).
      3. Our lives should be a festival of the unleavened bread of sincerity and truth (vv. 7, 8).
   E. In everyday life, it is impossible to avoid some contact with wicked men (vv. 9, 10).
   F. However, fellowship is forbidden with those who were in the church and have displayed wicked behavior (v. 11).
   G. God will judge those who are unbelievers (vv. 12a, 13a).
   H. We are responsible to judge those who profess to be believers, and to put them away from church and social fellowship when they are proved guilty (vv. 12b, 13b).

V. Lawsuits among believers (6:1-11).
   A. The inconsistency of believers taking their lawsuits before the unrighteous (vv. 1-5).

1. Believers will judge the world (v. 2).
2. Believers will judge angels (v. 3).
3. They should be able to judge things pertaining to this life (vv. 3, 4).
4. There should be at least one wise man in the local church (v. 5).
B. The wrong of believers going to law before believers (vv. 6-11).
   1. It is better to suffer wrong or be defrauded (v. 7).
   2. Instead of this, they were actually doing wrong and defrauding others (v. 8).
   3. People characterized by such conduct do not inherit the kingdom of God (vv. 9, 10).
   4. The Corinthians had been separated from sin and unrighteousness, and should not return to it (v. 11).

VI. Some principles for judging between right and wrong (6:12-20).
A. Some things are lawful but not expedient (v. 12).
B. Some are lawful but enslaving (v. 12).
C. Some are lawful but of temporary value only (v. 13).
D. Sexual impurity is utterly wrong (vv. 13-20).
   1. The body is for the Lord (v. 13).
   2. The Lord is for the body (v. 13).
   3. Our bodies will be raised (v. 14).
   4. Our bodies are members of Christ (vv. 15-17).
   5. Fornication is a sin against the body like no other sin (v. 18).
   6. The body is a temple of the Holy Ghost (v. 19).
   7. The body was purchased by Christ and belongs to God (v. 20).

SIN MUST BE JUDGED (5:1-8)

Chapter 5 deals with the necessity for disciplinary action in a church when one of its members has committed serious sin of public nature. Discipline is necessary that the church might retain its holy character before the eyes of the world and also so that the Holy Spirit might work ungrieved in its midst.

Apparently it had become widely known that one of the men in **5:1** the fellowship at Corinth had committed fornication. The word "fornication" is used here in its general sense as indicating sexual immorality. Here it was a very extreme form of sin, one that was not practiced even among the ungodly Gentiles. Specifically, the sin was that this man had had illicit intercourse with his father's wife. Perhaps the man's own mother had died and the father had married again. So his father's wife, in this case, would then refer to his step-mother. She was probably an unbeliever, because nothing is said about taking action against her. The church did not have jurisdiction in her case.

How had the Corinthian Christians reacted to all this? Instead of **5:2** plunging themselves into deep mourning, they were proud and haughty. Perhaps they were proud of their tolerance in not disciplining the offender. Or perhaps they were so proud of the abundance of spiritual gifts in the church that they did not give serious thought to what had taken place. They were not sufficiently shocked by sin.

"Ye have not rather mourned, that he that hath done this deed might be taken away from among you." This implies that if the believers had taken the proper attitude of humiliation before the Lord, He Himself would have acted in the matter, taking some form of disciplinary action on the offender. "They should have understood that the true glory of the Christian church consists not in the eloquence and gifts of its great teachers, but in the moral purity and the exemplary lives of its members"—Erdman.

In contrast to their indifference, the Apostle states that even **5:3** though he was absent, yet he had already judged the matter as if he were present. He pictures the church being assembled to take action **5:4** against the offender. Although he is not present bodily, yet he is there in spirit as they meet in the name of our Lord Jesus. The Lord Jesus had given authority to the church and to the apostles to exercise discipline in all such cases. Thus Paul says he would act with the power (or authority) of our Lord Jesus.

The action he would take would be *"to deliver such an one unto* **5:5** *Satan for the destruction of the flesh, that the spirit might be saved in the day of the Lord Jesus."* Commentators disagree on the meaning of this expression. Some feel that it describes the act of excommunication from the local church. Outside the church is the sphere of Satan's dominion (1 Jn. 5:19). Therefore, "to deliver unto Satan" would be simply to excommunicate from the church. Others feel that the

31

power to deliver unto Satan was a special power granted to apostles but no longer in existence today.

Again there is no agreement on the meaning of the expression "the destruction of the flesh." Many feel that it describes physical suffering that would be used of God to break the power of sinful lusts and habits in the man's life. Others feel that the destruction of the flesh is a description of slow death, which would give a man time to repent and be spared.

In any case, we should remember that the discipline of believers is always calculated to bring about their restoration to fellowship with the Lord. Excommunication is never an end in itself, but always a means toward an end. The ultimate purpose is "that the spirit may be saved in the day of the Lord Jesus." In other words, there is no thought of the man's eternal damnation. He is disciplined by the Lord in this life because of the sin he has committed but he is saved in the day of the Lord Jesus.

5:6   Paul now reproves the Corinthians for their glorying or boasting. Maybe they excused themselves by saying that it happened only once. They should have known that a little leaven leavens the whole lump. Leaven here is a picture of moral sin. The Apostle is saying that if they tolerate a little moral sin in the church, it will soon grow and expand until the whole fellowship is seriously affected. Righteous, godly discipline is necessary in order to maintain the character of the church.

5:7   Thus they are commanded to purge out the old leaven. In other words, they should take stern action against evil so that they might be a new, or better, "pure" lump. Then Paul adds, "Even as ye are unleavened." By this he means that, as to their standing before God, they are unleavened. God sees them in Christ as holy, righteous, and pure. Now the Apostle is saying that their state should correspond with their standing. As to *position* they were unleavened. Now as to their *practice* they should also be unleavened. Their natures should correspond with their name, and their conduct with their creed.

"For even Christ our passover is sacrificed for us." In thinking about the unleavened bread, Paul's mind goes back to the Passover Feast, where, on the eve of the first day of the Feast, the Jew was required to remove all leaven from his house. He went to the kneading trough and scraped it clean. He scrubbed the place where the leaven was kept till not a trace remained. He searched the house with a candle to

make sure that none had been overlooked. Then he lifted up his hands to God and said, "Oh God, I have cast out all the leaven from my house, and if there is any leaven that I do not know of, with all my heart I cast it out too." That pictures the kind of separation from evil to which the Christian is called in this day.

The slaying of the Passover lamb was a type or picture of the death of our Lord Jesus Christ on the Cross of Calvary. This verse is one of many in the New Testament that establishes the principle of typical teaching. By that we mean that persons and events of the Old Testament were types or shadows of things that were to come. Many of them pointed forward directly to the coming of the Lord Jesus to put away our sins by the sacrifice of Himself.

The feast in verse 8 does not refer to the Passover or to the Lord's **5:8** Supper but rather is used in a general way to describe the whole life of the believer. Our entire existence is to be a festival of joy, and it is to be celebrated not with the old leaven of sin nor with the leaven of malice and wickedness. "As we rejoice in our Savior, there must be no evil thoughts in our hearts toward our fellow-men"—Daily Notes. From this we see that the Apostle Paul was not speaking about literal leaven, such as the yeast that is used in making bread, but rather using leaven in a spiritual sense to describe the manner in which sin defiles that with which it comes in contact. We are to live our lives with the unleavened bread of sincerity and truth.

THOSE WITHOUT AND THOSE WITHIN (5:9-13)

Paul now explains to them that he had previously written in a letter **5:9** that they should have no company with fornicators. The fact that such an epistle is lost does not affect the inspiration of the Bible at all. It is not necessary to believe that every letter Paul ever wrote was inspired, but only those which God has seen fit to include in the Holy Bible.

The Apostle now goes on to explain that in warning them to have **5:10** no company with fornicators he did not mean to imply that they should separate themselves from any contact at all with ungodly men. As long as we are in the world, it is necessary for us to do business with unsaved people and we have no way of knowing the depths of sin to which they have descended. In order to live a life of complete isolation from sinners, one would have to go out of the world.

Paul says in this verse that he did not at all mean complete separation from the fornicators of this world or the covetous or the extortioners or idolaters. "Fornicators" refers to those who commit sexual immorality. Covetous men are those who are convicted of dishonesty in business or financial affairs. For instance, anyone who is found guilty of income tax fraud is subject to excommunication for covetousness. Extortioners are those who enrich themselves by using violent means, such as threats of harm or death. Idolaters are those who are given over to the worship of anyone or anything other than the true God, and who practice the terrible sins of immorality that are almost always connected with idolatry.

5:11 What Paul really wants to warn them against is having fellowship with a professing believer who engages in any of these terrible sins. We might paraphrase his words as follows: "What I meant to say and what I now repeat is that you should not even eat a common meal with any professing Christian who is a fornicator, or a covetous man, or an idolater, or a reviler, or a drunkard, or an extortioner."

It is often necessary for us to have contact with the unsaved, and we can oftentimes use these contacts in order to witness to them. Such contact is not as dangerous to the believer as having fellowship with those who profess to be Christians and yet who live in sin. We should never do anything that such a person might interpret as condoning his sin.

To the list of sinners mentioned in verse 10, Paul adds railers and drunkards in verse 11. A railer is a man who uses strong, intemperate language against another. But we would add a word of caution here. Should a man be excommunicated from the church if on one occasion only he should lose his temper and use unguarded words? We would think not but would suggest that this expression refers to habitual practice. In other words, a railer would be one who is known as being characteristically abusive toward others. At any rate, this should be a warning to us to exercise control of our language. As Dr. Ironside has mentioned, many people say that they are just *careless* with their tongue, but he points out that they might just as well say that they are careless with a machine gun.

Drunkards, of course, are those who are given to excess in the use of alcoholic beverages.

Does the Apostle Paul mean that we are not to eat with Christians who engage in these practices? That is exactly what the verse teaches.

34

We are not to eat with them at the Lord's Supper, nor are we to enjoy a social meal with them. There may be exceptional cases. A Christian wife, for instance, would still be obligated to eat with her husband who had been disfellowshipped. But the general rule is that professing believers who are guilty of the sins listed should be subjected to social ostracism in order to impress on them the enormity of their transgression and to bring them to repentance. If it be objected that the Lord ate with publicans and sinners, we would point out that these men did not profess to be His followers, and in eating with them He did not recognize them as His disciples. What this passage teaches is that we should not recognize as Christians men who are living wicked lives.

Paul's two questions in verse 12 mean that Christians are not **5:12** responsible for the judgment of those who are unsaved. Wicked men in the world about us will be brought into judgment by the Lord Himself in a coming day. But we do have a responsibility as far as judging those who are within the confines of the church. It is the duty of the local church to exercise godly discipline.

Again if it be objected that the Lord taught, "Judge not that ye be not judged," we would reply that there He is speaking about motives. We are not to judge men's motives because we are not competent for that type of judgment. We cannot tell their motives or read them. But the Word of God is equally clear that we are to judge known sin in the assembly of God so as to maintain its reputation for holiness and so as to restore the offending brother to fellowship with the Lord.

Paul explains that God will take care of the judgment of those that **5:13** are without, that is, of the unsaved. In the meantime, the Corinthians should exercise the judgment which God has committed to them by putting away the wicked man from among themselves. This would call, of course, for a public announcement in the church that this brother was no longer considered to be in fellowship. The announcement would be made in genuine sorrow and humiliation and would be followed by continual prayer for the spiritual restoration of the wanderer.

THE CHRISTIAN AND THE LAW (6:1-11)

The first eleven verses of this chapter have to do with lawsuits among believers. News had come to the Apostle Paul that some of the Christians were going to law against their fellow believers—before the judges of this world. He thereupon lays down these instructions of lasting value for the church. Note the repetition of the expression "Know ye not" (vv. 2, 3, 9, 15, 16, 19).

6:1 The opening question expresses shocked surprise that any of them would think of taking a brother to law before the unjust, that is, before unsaved judges or magistrates. He finds it rather inconsistent that those who know true righteousness should go before men who are not characterized by righteousness. "Imagine Christians going to seek justice from those who have none to give!"

6:2 A second glaring inconsistency is that those who will one day judge the world should be incapable of judging trivial matters that come up among themselves. The Scriptures everywhere teach that believers will reign with Christ over the earth when He returns in power and great glory, and that matters of judgment will be committed to them. If Christians are going to judge the world, should they not be able to handle petty differences that plague them now?

6:3 Paul reminds the Corinthians that they will judge angels. It is almost astounding to consider the manner in which the Apostle Paul injects such a momentous statement into the discussion. Without fanfare or build-up, he states the tremendous fact that Christians will one day judge angels. We know from Jude 6 and 2 Peter 2:4, 9 that angels will be judged. We also know that Christ will be the Judge (John 5:22). It is because of our union with Him that we can be spoken of as judging angels in a coming day. If we are considered qualified to judge angels, we should be able to handle the everyday problems that arise in life.

6:4 Verse 4 is very difficult to understand in the King James Version. It would seem as though the Apostle Paul were telling the Corinthians to take the least qualified or least esteemed men in the church and commit the matter of judgment to them. We do not believe that to be his thought at all. We will better understand the verse if we make the last clause a question instead of a statement: "If then ye have to judge things pertaining to this life, do ye set them to judge who are of no account in the church?" Unsaved judges are not given places of honor or esteem in the local church. They are, of course, respected for the work they are doing in the world, but as far as church matters are concerned they do not have any jurisdiction.

Thus Paul is asking the Corinthians, "When matters arise between you requiring the impartial judgment of some third party, do you go outside the confines of the church and set men to judge you who are not recognized by the church for spiritual discernment?"

Paul states that he asks this question to move them to shame. Is it 6:5 true that in an assembly that boasted of its wisdom and of the rich bestowment of gifts upon its members, not one wise man could be found to settle these quarrels among the brethren? Apparently not 6:6 one such wise man was available, since a Christian brother was going to law against his own brother in Christ, taking family matters before the unbelieving world. This was truly a deplorable situation.

But now Paul is going to press the matter a step further. They were 6:7 wrong even in going to law one against another. The expression "Now therefore there is utterly a fault among you," really means "you are entirely wrong in this thing." They shouldn't even think of going to law against one another. But perhaps one of the Christians would object at this point, "Paul, you don't understand. Brother so and so cheated me in business dealings." Paul's answer is, "Why not rather take wrong? Why not rather be defrauded?" This would be the truly Christian attitude to take. It is much better to receive a wrong than it is to commit one. But this was not the attitude among the 6:8 Corinthians. Instead of being willing to accept wrong and to be defrauded, they were actually committing wrong and were defrauding others, even their own brothers in Christ.

Had they forgotten that people whose lives are characteristically 6:9 unrighteous do not inherit the kingdom of God? If they have forgotten, then he will remind them of a list of sinners who will have no part in God's kingdom. He does not mean to imply that Christians can practice such sins and be lost, but rather he is saying that people who practice such sins are not Christians.

In this list, fornicators are distinct from adulterers. Here fornication would mean illicit sexual intercourse on the part of an unmarried person, whereas adultery would mean such conduct on the part of a married person. Idolaters are mentioned again, as in the two previous lists, in chapter 5. Then Paul lists "effeminate" and "abusers of themselves with mankind." The "effeminate" are those who allow their bodies to be used homosexually, while the "abusers of themselves with mankind" are those who practice sodomy on others. The "effeminate" are male prostitutes.

37

6:10 To the list is added thieves, covetous, drunkards, revilers, and extortioners. Thieves, of course, are those who take that which does not belong to them. Notice that the sin of covetousness is always listed among the most wicked vices. Though men might excuse it and think lightly of it, God condemns it vigorously. A covetous man is one with an inordinate desire for possessions that drives him to use unjust means of acquiring the same. Drunkards, as has been said, are those who are addicted to the use of drinks. Revilers are those who use abusive speech against others. Extortioners are those who take advantage of others' poverty or necessities to secure exorbitant gain.

6:11 Paul does not mean to imply that these sins were practiced by the Corinthian believers, but he is simply warning them that such things characterized them in the days before they were saved—"such were some of you." But they had been washed and sanctified and justified. They had been washed from their sin and impurity through the precious blood of the Lord Jesus Christ, and they were being continually washed from defilement through the Word of God. They were sanctified by the operation of the Spirit of God, being set apart to God from the world. They had been justified in the Name of the Lord Jesus Christ and in the Spirit of God; that is, they had been reckoned righteous before God on the basis of the work of the Lord Jesus on the Cross for them. What is Paul's argument here? It is simply this, as so aptly expressed by Godet, "Such a fathomless depth of grace is not to be recrossed."

HOW TO JUDGE RIGHT FROM WRONG (6:12-20)

6:12 In the concluding verses of this chapter, the Apostle Paul is going to lay down some principles for judging between right and wrong, principles that apply particularly to the matter of fleshly abuses. The first principle is this, that a thing may be lawful and yet it might not be expedient or helpful. When the Apostle says all things are lawful for me, he does not mean all things in an absolute sense. For instance, it would not be lawful for him to commit any of the sins mentioned above. We must remember that he is here speaking only about those things that are morally indifferent. For instance, the question as to whether a Christian should eat beef or pork was a very real issue among believers in the time of the Apostle Paul. Actually, it was a matter of moral indifference. It did not really matter to God

38

whether a man ate beef or pork. Paul is simply saying that certain things might be legitimate and yet they might not be profitable. There might be certain things which would be permissible for me to do and yet if someone else saw me doing them, he might be stumbled by my action. In such a case, it would not be at all expedient for me to do it. The word "expedient" is sometimes used in a bad sense today. For example, we speak of a man who is guided by expediency as an opportunist, doing whatever benefits him most without regard to what is right. But here in verse 12 the word means "profitable" or "suitable."

The second principle is that some things might be lawful and yet they might be enslaving. Paul states "I will not be brought under the power of any." This would have a very direct message today with regard to the subjects of liquor and tobacco. These things, as well as many others, are enslaving and the Christian should not allow himself to be thus put in bondage.

A third principle is that some things are perfectly lawful for the **6:13** believer and yet their value is temporary (verse 13). Paul says, "Meats for the belly, and the belly for meats: but God shall destroy both it and them." This means that the human stomach has been so constructed that it can receive food and digest it. It was made for the reception of food. Likewise, God has wonderfully designed food that it can be received by the human stomach. And yet we should not live for foods, because they are only of temporary value. They should not be given an undue place in the life of the believer. Someone has said, "Don't live as if your great business was the gratifying of your appetites."

Although the body is wonderfully designed by God for the reception and assimilation of food, there is one thing that is certain; the body is not for fornication but for the Lord, and the Lord for the body. In planning the human body, God never intended that it should be used for vile or impure purposes. Rather He planned that it should be used for the glory of the Lord and in His blessed service.

There is something amazing in this verse which should not escape the attention of the student. Not only is the body for the Lord, but even more wonderful is the thought that the Lord is for the body. This means that the Lord is interested in our bodies, in their welfare, and in their proper use. God wants our bodies to be presented to Him a living sacrifice, holy, and acceptable (Romans 12:1). As

Erdman says: "Without the Lord, the body can never attain its true dignity and its immortal destiny."

6:14 The fact that the Lord is for the body is further explained in this verse. God has not only raised the Lord Jesus from among the dead, but He will also raise us up through His power. His interest in our body does not end at the time of death. He is going to raise the body of every believer to fashion it like the glorious body of the Lord Jesus. We will not be disembodied spirits in eternity. Rather, our spirit and soul will be reunited with our glorified body, thus to enjoy the glories of heaven forever.

6:15 To further emphasize the necessity of personal purity in our lives and of the guarding of our bodies from impurity, the Apostle Paul reminds us that our bodies are members of Christ. In other words, every believer is a member of the body of Christ. Would it be proper, then, to take the members of Christ and make them the members of a harlot? To ask the question is to answer it, as Paul does with an indignant "God forbid."

6:16 In the act of sexual union, two bodies become one. It was so stated at the dawn of creation: "Two, saith he, shall be one flesh" (Genesis 2:24). This being so, if a believer should be joined to a harlot, it would be the same as making a member of Christ a member of a harlot. The two would become one flesh.

6:17 Just as in the physical act there is a union of two into one, so when a person believes on the Lord Jesus Christ and is joined to Him, the believer and Christ become so united that they can henceforth be spoken of as one spirit. This is the most perfect merging of two persons that is possible. It is the closest type of a union. Paul's argument, therefore, is that those who are thus joined with Christ should never tolerate any type of union that would be in conflict with this spiritual wedlock.

"The sheep may wander from the shepherd, and the branch be cut off from the vine; the member be severed from the body, the child alienated from the father, and even the wife from the husband; but when two spirits blend in one, what shall part them? No outward connection or union, even of wedlock, is so emphatically expressive of perfect merging of two lives in one"—A. T. Pierson.

6:18 And so the Apostle Paul warns the Corinthians to flee fornication. They are not to dabble with it, they are not to trifle with it, they are not to study it, to talk about it. They are to flee from it. A beautiful

40

Bible illustration of this is found in the case of Joseph when he was tempted to sin by the wife of Potiphar (Genesis 39). "While it is often claimed that there is safety in numbers, there are times when there is more safety in exodus"—quoted in Wycliffe Bible Commentary.

Then the Apostle adds, "Every sin that a man doeth is without the body; but he that committeth fornication sinneth against his own body." Most sins that a man commits have no direct effect on his body, but fornication is unique in the sense that it does affect man's body directly: he reaps the consequences of his sin in his own body. The difficulty with the verse is that it says that *every* sin that a man commits is without the body. But we believe that the Apostle is speaking here in a comparative sense. While it is true that gluttony and drunkenness, for example, affect a person's body, most sins do not. And not even gluttony or drunkenness affect the body as directly, as extensively or as destructively as immorality. Sex outside the marriage relationship inevitably and irresistibly works havoc on the offender.

Again the Apostle would remind the Corinthians that theirs was a 6:19 holy and dignified calling. Had they forgotten that their bodies were a temple of the Holy Spirit? That is the solemn truth of Scripture, that every believer is indwelt by the Spirit of God, and He is the *Holy* Spirit. How could we ever think of taking a body in which the *Holy* Spirit dwells and using it for *vile* purposes?

And not only is our body the dwelling place of the Holy Spirit, but in addition, the Apostle reminds us that we are not our own. It is not for us to take our bodies and use them the way we desire. In the final analysis they do not belong to us; they belong to the Lord.

We are the Lord's both by creation and redemption. Here the 6:20 latter is particularly in view. His ownership of us dates back to Calvary. We were bought with a price. At the Cross, we see the price-tag which the Lord Jesus put upon us. He thought us to be of such value that He was willing to pay for us with the price of His own precious blood. "How greatly Jesus must have loved me to bear my sins in His body on the tree."

That being the case, I can no longer think of my body as my own. If I am to take it and use it in the way I desire, then I am acting as a thief, taking that which does not belong to me. Rather I must use my body to glorify God, the One to whom it belongs.

41

"Head! Think of Him whose brow was thorn-girt. Hands! Toil for Him whose hands were nailed to the cross. Feet! Speed to do His behests whose feet were pierced. Body of mine! Be His temple whose body was wrung with pains unspeakable"—Bates.

When you have mastered this lesson, take the first part of Exam 2 (covering lesson 3), questions 1-10 on pages 13-15.

The Question of Marriage (7:1-40)

OUTLINE

VII. Instructions concerning marriage and celibacy (7:1-40).
  A. The unmarried state is good (v. 1).
  B. Marriage, however, is generally advisable because of the danger of moral impurity (vv. 2-6).
    1. Marriage should be to one person (v. 2).
    2. Each one should render to his partner the obligations of married life, since there is a mutual dependence (vv. 3, 4).
    3. The only exception is refraining from the marriage act to give one's self undividedly to prayer (vv. 5, 6).
      a. This refraining must be of temporary duration (v. 5).
      b. It must be by mutual consent (v. 5).
      c. It is permitted but not commanded (v. 6).
  C. Advice to the unmarried (vv. 7-9).
    1. Paul considers the unmarried state preferable, but recognizes that it can only be followed as God enables (v. 7).
    2. He advises the unmarried and widows to remain so (v. 8).
    3. However, he admits that marriage is preferable to lack of self-control (v. 9).
  D. Advice to married couples, where both partners are believers (vv. 10, 11).

1. The marriage tie is not to be broken (v. 10).
2. If separation takes place, there must be no remarriage, but rather reconciliation (v. 11).

E. Advice to a Christian whose partner is an unbeliever (vv. 12-24).
   1. Separation should not be considered by the believer (vv. 12-13), since the unbeliever is sanctified by the believer (v. 14).
   2. If the unbeliever desires to depart, he should be permitted to do so peacefully, but the hope of his eventual salvation should be ever present (vv. 15, 16).
   3. The general rule is that becoming a Christian need not involve violent revolution against existing ties (vv. 17-24).
      a. The principle illustrated as to racial ties (vv. 17-20).
      b. The principle illustrated as to social ties (vv. 20-24).

F. Advice to the unmarried, whether male or female (vv. 25-38).
   1. In general, it is good to be unmarried, in view of the present distress (vv. 25-28).
      a. This does not mean that married people should seek to be separated (vv. 25-27).
      b. Nor does it mean that it is a sin to marry (v. 28), even with all the troubles that go with it (v. 28).
   2. A second reason that favors the unmarried state is the shortness of time (vv. 29-31).
   3. A third reason is that the unmarried can better serve the Lord without distraction (vv. 32-35).
   4. If a man behaves unseemly toward his virginity, he is permitted to marry (v. 36).
   5. If a man can exercise self-control and maintain his virginity, he is better off (vv. 37, 38).

G. Advice to widows (vv. 39, 40).
   1. Death breaks the marriage bond, and a widow is free to remarry (v. 39).
   2. She is happier, however, to remain a widow (v. 40).

SHOULD A CHRISTIAN MARRY? (7:1-6)

7:1 Up to this point in the epistle, Paul has been dealing with various abuses that existed in the church at Corinth and which he had heard of by direct report. Now he is about to answer questions which the saints at Corinth sent to him. The first has to do with the subject of marriage and the single state. He therefore first lays down the broad principle that it is good for a man not to touch a woman. To touch a woman, in this case, means to marry. By this the Apostle does not imply that the unmarried state is a holier position than marriage, but simply that it is better to be unmarried if one desires to give himself to the service of the Lord without distraction. This will be explained in later verses.

The Apostle recognizes, however, that the single state carries with **7:2** it tremendous temptations to moral impurity. Thus he qualifies the first statement by saying, "To avoid fornication, let every man have his own wife, and let every woman have her own husband." To avoid fornication here means to avoid falling into sexual sin. For each man to have his own wife means that he is not to practice polygamy. Verse 2 establishes the principle that God's order for His people continues to be what it always was, namely, that a person should have only one wife or husband.

In the married state, each one should render to his partner the **7:3** obligations of married life, since there is a mutual dependence. When it says, "Let the husband render unto the wife due benevolence," it means, "Let him carry out his obligations to her as a husband." She should, of course, do likewise to him. As someone has said, "Note the delicacy which Paul uses in this section. There is no coarseness, crudeness, or vulgarity. How different this is from the world!"

In verse 4 we have the simple statement that in marital union there **7:4** is a dependence of the wife upon the husband and vice versa. In order to carry out God's order in this holy union, both husband and wife must recognize their interdependence. "In plain language this **7:5** means that if one partner desires the sexual relationship, the other should respond to that desire. The husband and wife who adopt this down-to-earth approach to sex will find it a wonderfully satisfying aspect of their marriage—for the simple reason that the relationship is rooted in reality, and not in some artificial or impossible ideal"— Larry Christenson. Perhaps when some of these Corinthians were first saved, they began to think that the intimacies of married life were not consistent with Christian holiness. Paul will disabuse their minds of any such idea. Here he firmly tells them that Christian couples are not to defraud one another, i.e., to deny one partner's rights as far as the other partner's body is concerned. There are only two exceptions. First of all, such an abstinence should only be by mutual consent so that the husband and wife might give themselves to prayer. Here it should be noticed that the word "fasting," as found in the Authorized Version, is omitted in many other versions of the Bible. The second condition is that such abstinence should only be temporary. Husband and wife should come together again, lest Satan tempt them for their incontinency.

7:6   The Apostle's words in verse 6 have given rise to a great deal of speculation and controversy. He says, "But I speak this by permission, and not of commandment." Some have taken this to mean that the Apostle did not consider the foregoing words to be inspired by God. Such an interpretation is untenable, since he claims in 1 Corinthians 14:37 that the things he was writing to the Corinthians were the commandments of the Lord. We feel rather that verse 6 refers to the subject immediately preceding it. The Apostle Paul was saying that under certain circumstances, it was all right for a married couple to abstain from the marriage act. He now adds that this abstinence is a permission but not a commandment. Christian people do not have to refrain from this act in order to give themselves undividedly to prayer. But they are allowed to do so by mutual consent and for a temporary period. Others feel that verse 6 refers to the whole idea of marriage, that is, that Christians are permitted to marry but are not commanded to do so.

ADVICE TO THE UNMARRIED (7:7-9)

7:7   Paul now begins advice to the unmarried. It is clear, first of all, that Paul considered the unmarried state to be preferable, but he recognized that it could be followed only as God enabled. When he says, "I would that all men were even as I myself," it is quite obvious from the context that he means "unmarried." There is much diversity of opinion as to whether Paul had always been a bachelor, or whether he was a widower at the time he wrote this verse. However, for present purposes, it is not necessary for us to settle the debate, even if we could. Where Paul says, "Every man has his proper gift of God, one after this manner, and one after that," he means that God gives

46

grace to some to remain unmarried whereas He definitely calls others to the married state. It is an individual matter, and no general legislation can be adopted which can be applicable to all. Therefore **7:8** he advises the unmarried and widows to remain even as he is himself. However, if they lack the power of self-control in the unmarried **7:9** state, then they are permitted to marry. "For it is better to marry than to burn." To burn here of course means to be consumed with passionate desire, followed by the very grave danger of falling into sin.

ADVICE TO MARRIED COUPLES (7:10-24)

1. Where Both Are Believers (7:10-11)

As pointed out previously the next two verses are addressed to mar- **7:10** ried couples, where both partners are believers. Verse 10 has been taken to imply that what Paul has written here is not inspired. He says, "Unto the married I command, yet not I, but the Lord." However, this simply means that what Paul was teaching here had already been taught by the Lord Jesus when He was on earth. Christ had already given an explicit command on this subject. For instance, He had forbidden divorce except on the ground of unfaithfulness (Matthew 5:32; 19:9; Mark 10:11; Luke 16:18). The over-all instruction that Paul gives is that a woman should not depart from her husband.

However, he recognizes that there are extreme cases where it **7:11** might be necessary for a wife to leave her husband. In such a case, she is obligated to remain unmarried, or to be reconciled to her husband. Separation does not break the marriage tie; rather it gives opportunity for the Lord to heal up the differences that have come between and to restore both parties to fellowship with Him and with one another. The husband is commanded not to leave his wife. No exception is made in his case.

2. Where One Partner Is Unsaved (7:12-24)

Verses 12 through 24 deal with the problem of a marriage where **7:12** only one party is a believer. Paul prefaces his remarks with the statement, "But to the rest speak I, not the Lord." Again, we would strongly emphasize that this does not mean that what Paul is saying represents his own viewpoint and not the Lord's. He is simply explaining that what he is about to say had not been previously taught by the Lord Jesus when He was here on the earth. There is no instruction in the Gospels similar to this. The Lord Jesus simply did not take up the case of a marriage where only one member was a believer. But now Christ had instructed His Apostle in this matter and so what Paul says here is the inspired Word of God.

The expression "but to the rest" means to those whose partners are not believers. This passage does not condone a Christian's marrying an unsaved person. It probably has in view the situation where one of the partners was saved after marriage.

"If any brother hath a wife that believeth not, and she be pleased to dwell with him, let him not put her away." In order to appreciate this passage of Scripture properly, it is helpful to remind ourselves of God's commandment to His people in the Old Testament. When Jews married heathen wives and had children by them, they were commanded to put both the wives and the children away. This is clearly seen in Ezra 10:2, 3 and Nehemiah 13:23-25.

Now the question has arisen in Corinth as to what a wife who had been converted should do about her husband and children, or what a man who has an unbelieving wife should do with her. Should he put her away? The answer is obviously negative. The commandment of the Old Testament no longer applies to the people of God under grace. If a Christian has a non-Christian wife and she is content to dwell with him, he should not leave her. This does not mean that it is all right for a man to marry a non-believer, but simply that being married to her, he is not obligated to leave her.

7:13   Likewise, a woman who has a non-Christian husband who is willing to live with her and to support her should stay with her husband. Perhaps by her meek and godly testimony before him, she will win him to the Lord.

7:14   Actually the presence of a believer in a non-Christian home has a sanctifying influence. As we have mentioned before, to sanctify means to set apart. Here it does not mean that the unbelieving husband is saved by his wife, neither does it mean that he is made holy. Rather it means that he is set apart in a position of external privilege. He is fortunate to have a Christian wife who bows the knee and prays for him. Her life and testimony are an influence for God in the home. Speaking from a human point of view, the likelihood of that man being saved is greater when he has a godly, Christian wife,

48

than if he had an unbelieving wife. "He receives a spiritual influence holding the possibility of actual conversion"—Vine. The same would hold true, of course, in the case of an unbelieving wife and a Christian husband. The unbelieving wife would be sanctified in such a case.

Then the Apostle adds, "Else were your children unclean; but now are they holy." We have already mentioned that in the Old Testament the children were to be put away as well as the heathen wife. Now Paul explains that in the dispensation of grace children born of a marriage where one partner is a believer and the other is not are holy. The word "holy" comes from the same word which was translated "sanctified" previously in this verse. It does not at all mean that the children are made holy in themselves, that is, that they necessarily live clean and pure lives. Rather it means that they are set apart in a place of privilege. They have at least one parent who loves the Lord, and who tells them the gospel story. There is a strong possibility of their being saved. They are privileged to live in a home where one of the parents is indwelt by the Spirit of God. In this sense, they are "sanctified." Of course, this verse also includes the assurance that it is not wrong to have children when one parent is a Christian and the other is not. God recognizes the marriage, and the children are not illegitimate.

But what should be the attitude of a Christian if the unsaved **7:15** partner desires to leave? The answer is that he should be allowed to leave. The expression "a brother or sister is not under bondage in such cases" (verse 15) is very difficult to explain with finality. Some believe that it means that if the unbeliever deserts the believer, and there is every reason to believe that the desertion is final, then the believer is free to obtain a divorce and to remarry. Those who hold this view teach that verse 15 is a parenthesis, and that verse 16 is connected with verse 14 as follows:

a. Verse 14 states that the ideal situation is for a believer to remain with an unbelieving partner because of the sanctifying influence of a Christian in the home.
b. Verse 16 suggests that through staying in the home, the believer may win the unbeliever to Christ.
c. Verse 15 is a parenthesis, allowing the believer to be divorced and to remarry if he or she is deserted by the unbeliever.

The hope of eventual salvation is connected with continued union

49

rather than with the unbeliever's leaving the home.

But other Bible students insist that verse 15 deals only with the subject of separation and not with divorce and remarriage. To them, it simply means that if the unbeliever departs, he should be allowed to do so peacefully. The wife is not under any obligation to keep the marriage together beyond what she has already done. God has called us in peace, and we are not required to use emotional displays or legal processes to prevent the unbeliever from departing.

Which is the right interpretation? We find it impossible to decide definitely. It does seem clear to us that the Lord taught in Matthew 19:9 that divorce is permitted where one party has been guilty of unfaithfulness (adultery or fornication). We believe that in such a case, the innocent person is free to remarry. As far as 1 Corinthians 7:15 is concerned, we cannot be positive that it permits divorce and remarriage where an unbeliever has deserted his Christian partner. However, we realize that anyone who is guilty of this form of desertion will almost inevitably enter into a new marriage very soon, and thus the original union will be broken anyway. J. W. Davies writes, "The unbeliever who departs would very soon be married to another, which would automatically break the marriage bond. To insist that the deserted party remain unmarried would put a yoke upon him/her which in the majority of cases, they would not be able to bear."

7:16   As explained above, one's understanding of verse 16 varies somewhat depending on his interpretation of verse 15.

If a person believes that verse 15 does not sanction divorce, he points to this verse as proof. He argues that the believer should permit separation but should not divorce the unbeliever because that would forever prevent the possibility of the restoration of the marriage union and the likelihood of the unbeliever's being saved. If, on the other hand, a person believes that divorce is permitted when a believer has been deserted, then this verse is linked with verse 14, and verse 15 is considered as a parenthesis.

7:17   There is often a very strong feeling among those who are newly converted that they must make a complete break with every phase of their former life, including institutions such as marriage which are not in themselves sinful. In the new-found joy of salvation, there is the danger of using forcible revolution to overthrow all that one has previously known. Actually, of course, Christianity does not use forcible revolution in order to accomplish its purposes. Rather, its changes are made by peaceful means. In verses 17 to 24 the Apostle Paul lays down the general rule that becoming a Christian need not involve violent revolution against existing ties. Doubtless he has marriage ties primarily in view, but he also applies the principle to racial ties and social ties.

Each one who is a believer is to walk in accordance with the calling of the Lord. If He has called one to married life, then he should follow this in the fear of the Lord. If God has given grace to live a celibate life, then a man should follow that calling. In addition, if at the time of a person's conversion, he is married to an unsaved wife, then he need not overturn this relationship, but should continue to the best of his ability to seek the salvation of his wife. What Paul is stating to the Corinthians is not for them alone; this is what he taught in all the churches. "When Paul says, 'and so ordain I in all the churches,' he is not issuing decrees from a given center, but is simply informing the Church at Corinth that the instructions he was giving them were what he gave in every church"—W. E. Vine.

Paul deals with the subject of racial ties in verses 18 and 19. If a **7:18** man were a Jew at the time of his conversion, and bore in his body the mark of circumcision, he need not take a violent revulsion at this and seek to obliterate all physical marks of his former way of life. Likewise if a man were a heathen at the time of his new birth, he does not have to let the pendulum swing to the other extreme and seek to hide his heathen background by taking on him the marks of a Jew.

We might also interpret this verse to mean that if a Jew were converted, he should not be afraid to live on with his Jewish wife, or if a Gentile were converted he should not try to flee from that background. These external differences are not what really count.

As far as the essence of Christianity is concerned, circumcision is **7:19** nothing and uncircumcision is nothing. What really counts is the keeping of the commandments of God. In other words, God is concerned with what is inward, not with what is outward. The relationships of life need not be violently sundered by the entrance of Christianity. "Rather, by the Christian faith, the believer is raised to a position where he is superior to all circumstances"—Kelly.

The general rule is that each man should abide in that calling **7:20** wherein he was called. This, of course, only refers to callings that are

51

not in themselves sinful. If a man were engaged in some wicked business at the time of his conversion, then, of course, he would be expected to leave it. But the Apostle here is dealing with things which are not in themselves wrong. This is proved in the following verses where the subject of bondservants is discussed.

7:21   What should a slave do when he is saved? Should he rebel against his owner? Should he demand his freedom? Does Christianity insist that we go about seeking our human rights? Paul gives the answer here, "Art thou called being a servant? Care not for it." In other words, "Were you a slave at the time of your conversion? Do not be needlessly concerned about that. You can be a slave and still enjoy the highest blessings of Christianity."

"But if thou mayest be made free, use it rather." There are two interpretations of this passage. Some feel that Paul is saying, "If you can become free, by all means avail yourself of this opportunity." Others feel that the Apostle is saying that even if a slave could become free, Christianity does not require him to avail himself of that freedom. Rather he should use his bondage as a testimony to the Lord Jesus Christ. Most students will prefer the first interpretation (and it is probably correct), but they should not overlook the fact that the second would be more nearly in accord with the example left to us by the Lord Jesus Christ Himself.

7:22   "He that is called in the Lord, being a servant, is the Lord's freeman." Here the word "freeman" should actually be "freedman." It does not mean a man who was freeborn but rather one who was made free, that is, a slave who obtained his freedom. In other words, if a man was a slave at the time of his conversion, he should not let that worry him, because he is the Lord's freedman. He has been set free from his sins and from the bondage of Satan. On the other hand, if a man were free at the time of his conversion, he should realize that he is henceforth a bondslave, bound hand and foot to the Savior.

7:23   Every Christian has been bought with a price. He henceforth belongs to the One Who bought him, the Lord Jesus. We are to be
7:24   Christ's bondslaves and not the bondslaves of men. Therefore, no matter what one's social state was, he can consistently remain in that state and abide in it with God. These last two words are the key which unlocks the whole truth. If a man is with God, then even slavery can be made true freedom. "It is that that ennobles and sanctifies any position in life."

52

MORE ADVICE TO THE UNMARRIED (7:25-38)

From verse 25 through verse 38, the Apostle is addressing himself to the unmarried, whether male or female. The word "virgin" can be used to apply to either.

Verse 25 is another verse that men have used to teach that the **7:25** contents of this chapter are not necessarily inspired. They even go to such extremes as to say that Paul, being a bachelor, was a male chauvinist and that his personal prejudices are reflected in what he says here. To adopt such an attitude, of course, is to deal a vicious attack on the inspiration of the Scriptures. When Paul says he has no commandment of the Lord concerning virgins, he simply means that during the Lord's earthly ministry He did not leave any explicit instruction on this subject. Therefore Paul gives his own judgment, as one who has received mercy of the Lord to be faithful, and this judgment is inspired of God.

In general, it is good to be unmarried, in view of the present **7:26** distress. The expression "present distress" refers to the sufferings of this earthly life in general. Perhaps there was a special time of distress at the time Paul wrote this letter. However, distress has continued to exist and will continue until the Lord comes. Paul's advice **7:27** in the first part of verse 27 is that those who are already married should not seek to be separated from that marriage. On the other hand, if a man is loosed from a wife, he should not seek a wife. The expression "to be loosed from a wife" here does not only mean widowed or divorced, as one would suspect. It simply means free from the marriage bond, and could include those who never married.

Nothing that Paul says should be construed to indicate that it is a **7:28** sin to marry. After all, marriage was instituted by God in the Garden of Eden before sin ever entered the world. It was God Himself who decreed, "It is not good for man to be alone" (Gen. 2:18). "Marriage is honorable in all, and the bed undefiled" (Heb. 13:4). Paul elsewhere speaks of those who forbid to marry as being a sign of latter-day apostasy (1 Tim. 4:1-3).

Thus Paul states, "If thou marry, thou hast not sinned; and if a virgin marry, she hath not sinned." New converts to Christianity should never think that there is anything inherently wrong in the marriage relationship. Yet Paul adds that those women who do marry will have trouble in the flesh. This may include the travail connected with childbirth, etc. When Paul says, "But I spare you," he may mean (1) I would spare you the physical suffering which accompanies the marriage state, particularly the troubles of family life, or (2) I would spare the reader the enumeration of all these troubles.

7:29   The thing that Paul would like to emphasize is this, that because of the shortness of the time, we should subordinate even these legitimate relationships of life in order to serve the Lord. The time of Christ's coming is near and although husbands and wives should perform their mutual duties with faithfulness, they should seek to put Christ first in all their lives. Ironside expresses it in this way: "Everyone is to act in view of the fact that the time is indeed fleeting, the Lord's return is nearing, and no consideration of personal com-
7:30   fort is to be allowed to hinder devotion to the will of God." The sorrows and joys and possessions of life should not be given a place of undue consideration in our lives. All these must be subordinated in our endeavor to buy up the opportunity to serve the Lord while it is still day.

7:31   In living our lives on the earth, it is inevitable that we have a certain amount of contact with mundane things. There is a legitimate use of these things in the life of the believer. However, Paul warns that while we may use them, we should not abuse them. For instance, the Christian should not live for food and clothing and pleasure. He may use food and clothing as essentials but they should not become the god of his life. Marriage, property, commerce, or political, scientific, and artistic activity have their place in the world, but all may prove a distraction to spiritual life if allowed to do so.

The expression "the fashion of this world passeth away" is borrowed from the language of the theater and refers to the changing of scenes. It speaks of the transience of all that we see about us today. Its short-lived character is well expressed in the well-known words "All the world's a stage, and all the men and women merely players. They have their exits and their entrances, and one man in his time plays many parts"—Shakespeare.

7:32   Paul would have the Christians to be free from cares. He means, of course, cares that would unnecessarily hinder them from serving the Lord. And so he goes on to explain that he that is unmarried is careful for the things of the Lord, how he may please the Lord. This does not mean that all unmarried people do give themselves undistractedly to the Lord, but it means that the unmarried state provides the opportunity for so doing in a way that the married state does not. Again this does not mean that a married man cannot be very attend- **7:33** ive to the things of the Lord, but it is a general observation that married life requires that a man take an interest in the things of his wife. He has additional obligations to think of. As Vine has pointed out, "In general, if a man is married, he has limited his range of service. If he is unmarried, he can go to the ends of the earth and preach the gospel."

In the King James Version, verse 34 begins with the statement, **7:34** "There is difference also between a wife and a virgin." In the New American Standard Bible, the verse begins, "and *his interests* are divided." Thus in the New American Standard Bible, verses 33 and 34 are connected as follows: "but one who is married is concerned about the things of the world, how he may please his wife, and his interests are divided." In other words, his time and attention are divided between his wife and the service of the Lord.

"And the woman who is unmarried, and the virgin, is concerned about the things of the Lord, that she may be holy both in body and spirit; but one who is married is concerned about the things of the world, how she may please her husband" (NASB). A word of explanation is needed here also. The unmarried woman, or the virgin, is able to give a greater portion of her time to the things of the Lord. The expression, "that she may be holy both in body and spirit," does not mean that the unmarried state is more holy, but it simply means that she can be more set apart in both body and spirit to the work of the Lord. She is not essentially purer, but her time is freer.

Again, "one who is married is concerned about the things of the world." That does not mean that she is more worldly than the unmarried woman, but simply that her day must necessarily be devoted in part to mundane duties such as care of the home. These things are legitimate and right, and Paul is not criticizing them or depreciating them; he is merely stating that an unmarried woman has wider avenues for service and more time than the one who is married.

Paul is not setting forth this teaching in order to put people under **7:35** a rigid system of bondage. He is merely instructing them for their own profit so that when they think of their lives and of the service of the Lord, they may judge His guidance in the light of all this instruction. His attitude is that celibacy is comely, or seemly, and enables a person to attend upon the Lord without distraction. As far as Paul is concerned, man is free to choose either marriage or celibacy. Paul does not want to cast a snare upon anyone or to put them into bondage.

Verses 36 through 38 are perhaps the most misunderstood verses in this chapter, and perhaps in the entire epistle. The common explanation is this. In the days of the Apostle Paul, a man exercised a very rigid control over his home. It was up to him whether his daughters married or not. They could not do so without his permission. Thus these verses are taken to mean that if a man refuses to allow his daughters to marry, that is a good thing, but if he allows them to marry, then he is not sinning. Frankly the writer finds such an interpretation to be almost meaningless as far as instruction for the people of God in this day is concerned. The interpretation does not fit in with the context of the rest of the chapter, and seems to be hopelessly confusing.

The Revised Standard Version translates "virgin" as "betrothed." The thought seems to be that if a man marries his betrothed or fiancee, he does not sin; but if he refrains from marrying her, it is better. Such a view is laden with difficulties.

In his commentary on 1 Corinthians, William Kelly presents an alternate view which seems to the writer to have great merit. He shows that the word "virgin" may also be translated "virginity," and that the passage is not speaking about a man's virgin daughters, but about his own virginity. According to this interpretation, what the passage is saying is that if a man maintains the unmarried state he does well, but that if he decides to get married, he does not sin.

John Nelson Darby adopts this same interpretation in his New Translation of the Bible. Perhaps we would do well to quote his translation of these verses at this point: "But if any one think that he behaves unseemly to his virginity, and if he is beyond the flower of his age, and so it must be, let him do what he will, he does not sin: let them marry. But he who stands firm in his heart, having no need, but has authority over his own will, and has judged this in his heart to keep his own virginity, he does well. So that he that marries himself does well: and he that does not marry does better."

Looking at verse 36 in greater detail then, we take it as meaning that if a man has passed full manhood, and if he does not feel that he has the gift of continence, he does not do wrong in marrying. He feels that need requires him to do so, and so he should do what he

wishes in this case. However, if a man has determined to serve the 7:37
Lord undistractedly, and if he has sufficient self-control so that there
is no necessity for his marrying, if he has determined to maintain the
unmarried state, and this with a view to glorifying God in service,
then he does well. The conclusion is that the one who gives himself 7:38
in marriage does well, but that the one who maintains the unmarried
state for greater service for the Lord does better.

The last two verses of the chapter contain advice to widows. A wife 7:39
is bound by the law to her husband as long as he lives. The law
referred to here is the marriage law, instituted by God. If a woman's
husband dies, she is at liberty to be married to another man. This
same truth is enunciated in Romans 7:1-3, namely, that death breaks
the marriage relationship. However, the Apostle Paul adds the qual-
ification that she is free to marry whom she will, "only in the Lord."
This means, first of all that the person she marries must be a Christian, but it means more than this. The expression "in the Lord"
means "in the will of the Lord." In other words, she might marry a
Christian and still be out of the will of the Lord. She must seek the
guidance of the Lord in this important matter and marry the believer
whom the Lord would have for her.

Paul's frank judgment is that a widow would be happier if she 7:40
remained unmarried. This does not contradict 1 Timothy 5:14 where
Paul expresses his judgment that younger widows should marry.
Here he is stating the general idea. In 1 Timothy he gives a specific
exception.

Then he adds the words "I think also that I have the Spirit of
God." Many understand these words to mean that Paul was not sure
of himself in stating these things. Again we protest vigorously against
any such interpretation. There can be no question as to the inspiration of what Paul wrote in this portion. We believe that he is using
irony here. His apostleship and his teaching had been under attack
by some at Corinth. They professed to have the mind of the Lord in
what they were saying. Paul is saying in effect, "Whatever else others
may say of me, I think that I also have the Spirit of God. They
profess to have it but surely they do not think that they have a
monopoly on the Spirit of God."

We know today that Paul did indeed have the Spirit in all that he
wrote to us, and that the path of blessedness for us is to follow his
instructions.

When you are ready, complete Exam 2 by answering questions 11-20 on pages 16-18 . (You should have already answered questions 1-10 as part of your study of Lesson 3.)

Lesson 5

Christian Liberty (8:1—9:27)

OUTLINE

VIII. The question of eating meats offered to idols (8:1—11:1).
    A. Knowledge alone is not a sufficient guide (vv. 1-3).
        1. Knowledge tends to beget pride (vv. 1, 2).
        2. Love is greatly needed (v. 3).
    B. The truth concerning idols (vv. 4-6).
        1. There are no real gods, such as idols are supposed to represent (v. 4).
        2. There are so-called gods, supposed to be in heaven and in earth—in fact there are many such mythological gods (v. 5).
        3. But there is only one true God and one true Lord Jesus Christ (v. 6).
    C. The danger of offending a weak brother by eating meats offered to idols (vv. 7-13).
        1. It is a small sacrifice to give up meats under such circumstances (vv. 7, 8).
        2. It is a serious thing to be a stumbling block to a weaker brother (vv. 9-12).
           a. It may encourage him to do what his conscience condemns (vv. 9, 10).
           b. In this way, his testimony is wrecked—one for whom Christ died (v. 11).
           c. Such is a sin against Christ (v. 12).
        3. It is better never to eat meat than to offend a brother (v. 13).

D. Paul's example of self-denial for the good of others (9:1-27).
1. Paul's claim to be an apostle (vv. 1-3).
   a. He had seen the Lord Jesus (v. 1a).
   b. The Lord had blessed his labors (vv. 1b-3).
2. Paul's right to financial support as an apostle (vv. 4-14).
   a. The example of other apostles (vv. 4-6).
   b. Argument from human affairs (v. 7).
      (1) Soldier.
      (2) Vineyard planter.
      (3) Shepherd.
   c. Argument from the law of Moses (vv. 8-11).
   d. Others were being supported by the Corinthians (v. 12).
   e. Argument from the support of those who served in the Jewish temple (v. 13).
   f. The definite command of the Lord Himself (v. 14).
3. Paul's reason for refusing this right of support (vv. 15-18).
   a. He could not boast in preaching the gospel, since this was a necessity (vv. 15-17).
   b. Therefore, he would glory in the fact that he supported himself financially in order to make the gospel without charge to others (v. 18).
4. Paul's example of waiving legitimate rights for the gospel's sake (vv. 19-23).
   a. With the Jews (v. 20).
   b. With those under the law (v. 20).
   c. With those not under law (v. 21).
   d. With the weak (v. 22).
   e. With all men (v. 22).
5. The peril of losing one's reward through lack of self-discipline (vv. 23-27).
   a. As athletes run to win the prize, so we should run to win (v. 24).
   b. As athletes practice self-discipline to obtain a corruptible crown, we should do the same to win an incorruptible crown (v. 25).
   c. Paul's example of discipline (vv. 26, 27).

(1) He did not run aimlessly (v. 26).
(2) He did not beat the air (v. 26).
(3) He kept his body in subjection (v. 27).
(4) He feared being disapproved at last (v. 27).

WE NEED MORE THAN KNOWLEDGE (8:1-3)

The question of eating meat offered to idols is taken up in chapter 8 and is continued through the first verse of chapter 11. This was a real problem to those who had recently been converted from heathenism to Christianity. Perhaps they would be invited to a social event at an idol temple where a great feast would be spread with meat that had previously been offered to the idols. Or perhaps they would go to the market place to buy meat and find that the butcher was selling meat that had been offered to idols. This would not affect the quality of the meat in any way, of course, but should the Christian buy it? Again, a believer might be invited to a home and be served food that had been offered up to some idol deity. If he knew that this had been the case, should he partake of the food? In the portion of Scripture before us, Paul addresses himself to answering these questions.

The Apostle begins by stating that as far as things offered to idols **8:1** were concerned, both the Corinthians and he himself had knowledge. It was not a subject about which they were completely ignorant. They all knew, for instance, that the mere act of offering a piece of meat to an idol had not changed it in any sense. Its flavor and nutritional value remained the same as they were before. However, Paul points out that knowledge puffs up, but love edifies. By this he means that knowledge in itself is not a sufficient guide in these matters. If knowledge were the only principle that were applied, then it might lead to pride. Actually in all such matters the Christian must use not only knowledge but love as well. He must not only consider what is lawful for himself, but what would be for the best interests of others.

Vine paraphrases verse 2 as follows: "If a man imagines he has fully **8:2** acquired knowledge, he has not even begun to know how it ought to be gained." Without love there can be no true knowledge. On the **8:3** other hand, if any man loves God, that man is known by God in the sense that he is approved by Him. In one sense, of course, God knows every man, and in another sense, He knows especially those who are believers. But here the word "know" is used to denote favor or approval. What this verse is saying is that if any man makes his decisions in such matters as meats offered to idols out of love to God and man and not out of mere knowledge, that person wins the smile of God's approval.

THE TRUTH ABOUT IDOLS (8:4-6)

8:4 As far as things offered to idols are concerned, believers understand that an idol is not a real god with power, knowledge, and love. Paul was not here denying the existence of idols themselves; he knew that there were such things as graven images, carved out of wood or stone. Later on he acknowledges that behind these idols there are demon powers. But what he here emphasizes is that the gods which these idols purport to represent do not exist. There is no god but one, that is the God and Father of our Lord Jesus Christ.

8:5 Paul admits that there were many so-called gods in heathen mythology, such as Jupiter, Juno, and Mercury. Some of these gods were supposed to live in heaven, and others, such as Ceres and Neptune, here on the earth. In this sense there are many gods and many lords, that is, mythological beings which people nonetheless worshiped and to which they were in bondage.

8:6 Believers know that there is one true God the Father, of whom are all things and we unto Him. This means that God, our Father, is the Source or Creator of all things and that we were created for Him, that is, He is the purpose or goal of our existence. We also know that there is one Lord, namely Jesus Christ, through whom are all things and we through Him. The expression "through whom are all things" describes the Lord Jesus as the mediator or agent of God, whereas the expression "we through Him" indicates that it is through Him that we have been created and redeemed.

When Paul says that there is one God, the Father, and one Lord Jesus Christ, he does not mean that the Lord Jesus Christ is not God. Rather he simply indicates the respective roles which these two persons of the Godhead fulfilled in creation and in redemption.

THE WEAKER BROTHER (8:7-13).

8:7 However, not all Christians, especially new converts, understand the liberty which they have in Christ Jesus. Having come from backgrounds of idolatry and being used to idols, they think that they are committing an act of idolatry when they eat meat that has been offered to idols. They think that the idol is a reality and therefore their conscience, being weak, is defiled.

When the Scripture uses the expression "weak," it does not mean physically weak or even spiritually weak. It is a term used to describe those who are unduly scrupulous in matters of moral indifference. For instance, as far as God is concerned, it is not wrong for a believer to eat pork. It would have been wrong for a Jew to do so in the Old Testament, but a Christian is at perfect liberty to partake of such food. However, a Jew converted to Christianity might still have scruples about this. He might feel it wrong to eat a roast pork dinner. He is what the Bible speaks of as a weak brother. It means that he is not living in the full enjoyment of his Christian liberty. Actually, as long as he thinks that it is wrong to eat pork, he would sin if he went ahead and did it. That is what is meant by the expression here, "their conscience being weak is defiled." If my conscience condemns a certain act and I go ahead and commit it, then I have sinned. "Whatsoever is not of faith is sin" (Rom. 14:23).

Food in itself is not a matter of great consequence to God. Refraining from certain foods does not give us favor with God, nor does the partaking of such foods make us better Christians. But although there is nothing to gain by eating these foods, there might be much to lose if in so doing I cause a weak Christian to stumble. This is where the principle of love must come in. A Christian has liberty to eat meat that has been previously offered in sacrifice to idols, but it would be utterly wrong for him to eat it if in so doing he offends a weak brother in Christ. **8:8** **8:9**

The danger is that the weak brother might be encouraged to do what his conscience condemns, if he sees another doing something which to him is questionable. In this verse, the Apostle condemns the practice of eating in an idol's temple because of the effect it would have on others. Of course, when Paul speaks here of eating in an idol's temple, he is referring to some social event or some general celebration, such as a wedding. It would never be right to eat in such a temple if the meal involved participation in idol-worship in any way. Paul later condemns that (10:15-26). **8:10**

The expression "for if any man see thee which hath knowledge" means if any man sees you, who have a full measure of Christian liberty, who know that meat offered to idols is not unclean or impure, etc. The important principle here is that we must not only consider what effect such an action would have upon ourselves, but even more important, what effect it would have upon others.

8:11   A man may so parade his knowledge of what is legitimate for a Christian as to cause a brother in Christ to stumble. The word "perish" does not mean that he would lose his eternal salvation. It means not the loss of *being* but the loss of *well-being*. This weak brother's testimony would be hurt and his life would be adversely affected as far as usefulness for God is concerned. The tremendous seriousness of so offending a weak brother in Christ is indicated by the closing words "for whom Christ died." Paul's argument is that if the Lord Jesus Christ loved this man to a sufficient extent that He was willing to die for him, we should not dare to hinder his spiritual progress by doing anything that would stumble him. A few slices of meat are not that important.

8:12   It is not just a matter of sinning against a brother in Christ, or of wounding his weak conscience. It constitutes sin against Christ Himself. Whatever we do to the least of His brothers we do to Him. What hurts one of the members of the body hurts the Head as well. Vine points out that in dealing with each subject, the Apostle leads his readers to view it in the light of the atoning death of Christ. Barnes adds, "It is an appeal drawn from the deep and tender love, the sufferings, and the dying groans of the Son of God." Sin against Christ is what Godet calls "the highest of crimes." Realizing this, we should be very careful to examine all our actions in the light of their effect on others, and to refrain from doing anything that would cause a brother to be offended.

8:13   Because it is sin against Christ to cause a brother to stumble, Paul states that he will eat no meat while the world stands if in doing so he makes his brother to offend. The work of God in the life of another person is far more important than a tender roast. Although the subject of meats offered to idols is not a problem for most Christians today, the principles which the Spirit of God gives us in this section are of abiding value. There are many things today in the Christian life, which, while they are not forbidden in the Word of God, would yet cause needless offense to weaker Christians. While we might have the right to participate in them, a greater right is to forego that right for the spiritual welfare of those we love in Christ.

PAUL'S EXAMPLE OF SELF DENIAL (9:1-27)

At first glance, chapter 9 might seem to indicate a new subject. However, as we go on, we shall find that the question of meats offered to idols continues for two more chapters. Paul is here merely turning aside to give his own example of self-denial for the good of others. He was willing to forego his right to support as an apostle in accordance with the principle set forth in 8:13. Thus this chapter is closely linked with that with which we have just been dealing.

1. His Apostolic Claim (9:1-3)

As we know, there were those in Corinth who questioned Paul's **9:1** authority. They said that he was not one of the twelve, and therefore was not a genuine apostle. Paul protests that he was free from human authority, a genuine apostle of the Lord Jesus. He bases his claim on two facts. First of all, he had seen Jesus, the Lord, in resurrection. This took place on the road to Damascus. He also points to the Corinthians themselves as proof of his apostleship by asking the question, "Are not ye my work in the Lord?" If they had any doubt as to his apostleship, they should examine themselves. Were they saved? Of course they would say that they were. Well, who pointed them to Christ? The Apostle Paul did. Therefore, they themselves were proof of the fact that he was a genuine apostle of the Lord. Others may not recognize him as an apostle, but surely the Corinthi- **9:2** ans themselves should. They were the seal of his apostleship in the Lord.

Verse 3 refers to what has gone before, and not to what follows. **9:3** Paul is saying that what he has just said is his defense to those who examine him, or who question his authority as an apostle.

2. His Right to Financial Support (9:4-14)

In verses 4 through 14, the Apostle discusses his right to financial **9:4** support as an apostle. As one who had been sent by the Lord Jesus, Paul was entitled to financial remuneration from the believers. However, he had not always insisted on this right. Oftentimes he had worked with his hands, making tents, in order that he might be able to preach the gospel freely to men and women. No doubt his critics took advantage of this, suggesting that the reason that he did not take support was that he knew that he was not a real apostle.

He introduces the subject by asking a question, "Have we not power to eat and to drink?" Here the word "power" means right or authority. Paul is asking, "Do we not have the right to be given food and drink without having to work for it? Are we not entitled to be supported by the church?"

9:5 Verse 5 is much clearer in the New American Standard Bible, where it reads, "Do we not have a right to take along a believing wife, even as the rest of the apostles, and the brothers of the Lord, and Cephas?" Again perhaps some of Paul's critics suggested that Paul did not marry because he knew he and his wife would not be entitled to the support of the churches. Peter and the other apostles were married, as were also the brothers of the Lord. The Apostle is here stating that he would have just as much right to be married and enjoy the support of the Christians for both his wife and himself. The expression "to lead about a wife that is a believer" refers not only to the right to marry, but also to the right of support for both husband and wife. The brothers of the Lord may mean His actual half brothers or His cousins. This text alone does not solve the problem, although other Scriptures seem to indicate that Mary did have other children after Jesus, her Firstborn (Luke 2:7). (See Mt. 1:25; 12:46; 13:55; Mk. 6:3; Jn. 2:12; Gal. 1:19).

9:6 It appears from verse 6 that Barnabas, like Paul, had worked to provide for his material needs while preaching the gospel. Paul asks if they both did not have the right to stop working and to be cared for by the people of God.

9:7 The Apostle based his first claim to financial support upon the example of the other apostles. He now turns to an argument from human affairs. Soldiers are not sent into a battle at their own expense. Those who plant vineyards are never expected to do so without receiving some recompense from the harvest. Finally, a shepherd is not expected to keep his flock without being given a right to partake of the milk. Christian service is like warfare, agriculture, and pastoral life. It involves fighting against the enemy, caring for God's fruit trees, and serving as an under-shepherd for His sheep. If the right of support is recognized in these earthly occupations, how much more should it be in the service of the Lord!!

9:8 The Apostle next turns to the Old Testament Scriptures for further proof of his point. Does he have to base his argument merely on

66

these mundane things of life, such as warfare, agriculture, and shepherding? Do not the Scriptures of the Old Testament say the same thing? It is clearly stated in Deuteronomy 25:4 that an ox **9:9** should not be muzzled when it treads out the grain. That is, when an animal is used in a harvesting operation, it should be allowed to partake of some of the harvest. Is it for the oxen that God careth? The answer is yes, God does care for oxen, but He didn't cause these things to be written in the Old Testament merely for the sake of dumb animals. There was a spiritual principle involved to be applied to our life and service.

"Or saith he it altogether for our sakes?" This means, "Doesn't **9:10** God say it assuredly for our benefit?" The answer is yes, our welfare was in His mind when these words were written. When a man plows, he should plow with the expectation of some remuneration. So likewise, when a man threshes, he should be able to look forward to some of the harvest in recompense. Christian service resembles plowing and threshing, and God has decreed that those who engage in these aspects of His service should not do so at their own charges.

Paul speaks of himself as having sowed spiritual things to the **9:11** Christians at Corinth. In other words, he came to Corinth preaching the gospel to them and teaching them precious spiritual truths. That being so, is it asking too much if in return they should minister to him of their finances or other material things? The argument is that "the wages of the preacher are greatly inferior in value to what he has given. Material benefits are small compared with spiritual blessings."

Paul was aware of the fact that the church at Corinth was support- **9:12** ing others who were preaching or teaching there. They recognized this obligation to these other men but not to the Apostle Paul, and so he asks, "If others be partakers of this power over you, are we not rather?" In other words, if they recognized the right of others to financial support, why should they not then recognize that he, their father in the faith, had this right? Doubtless those who were being supported were the Judaizing teachers. Paul adds that, though he had this right, he did not use it with the Corinthians but endured all things that he might cause no hindrance to the gospel of Christ. Rather than insist on his right to receive support from them, he bore all sorts of privations and hardships lest the gospel should be hindered.

Paul next introduces the argument from the support of those who **9:13**

67

served in the Jewish temple. Those who had official duties in connection with the temple service were supported from the income the temple received. In this sense they lived off the things of the temple. Also the priests themselves who served at the altar were given a certain portion of the offerings that were brought to the altar. In other words both the Levites, who had the ordinary duties around the temple, and the priests, to whom were entrusted the more sacred duties, were alike supported for their service.

9:14   Finally, Paul introduces the definite command of the Lord Himself. He ordained that they which preach the gospel should live by the gospel. This would be conclusive proof alone of Paul's right to support from the Corinthians. But this raises the question of why he did not insist on being supported by them. The answer is given in verses 15 through 18.

3. Why Paul Refused Financial Support (9:15-18)

9:15   He explains that he used none of these things, that is, he did not insist on his rights. Neither was he writing these things at the present time in order that they might send money to him. He would rather die than that anyone should be able to rob him of his boasting.

9:16   In verse 16, Paul is saying that he cannot boast in the fact that he preaches the gospel. A divine compulsion is placed upon him to preach the gospel. It is not a vocation that he chose for himself. He received the "tap on the shoulder" and he would have been a most miserable man if he had not obeyed the divine commission. This does not mean the Apostle was not willing to preach the gospel, but rather that the decision to preach did not come from himself, but from the Lord.

9:17   If the Apostle Paul preached the gospel willingly, then he would have the reward that goes with such service, namely, the right of maintenance. Throughout the Old and New Testaments, it is clearly taught that those who serve the Lord are entitled to support from the Lord's people. In this passage, Paul does not mean that he was an unwilling servant of the Lord, but is simply stating that there was a divine compulsion in his apostleship. He goes on to emphasize this in the latter part of the verse. If he preached against his will, that is, if he preached because there was a fire burning within him and he could not refrain from preaching, then a stewardship of the gospel was committed to him. He was a man acting under orders, and therefore he could not boast in that.

Verse 17 is admittedly difficult, and yet the meaning seems to be that Paul would not claim his right of maintenance from the Corinthians because the ministry was not an occupation which he chose by himself. He was placed in it by the hand of God. The false teachers in Corinth might claim their right to be supported by the saints, but the Apostle Paul would seek his reward elsewhere.

Knox's translation of this verse is as follows: "I can claim a reward for what I do of my own choice; but when I act under constraint, I am only executing a commission."

Ryrie comments, "Paul could not escape his responsibility to **9:18** preach the gospel, because a stewardship (responsibility) had been committed to him and he was under orders to preach even though he was never paid (cf. Luke 17:10)."

If then he could not boast in the fact that he preached the gospel, of what would he boast? Of something that was a matter of his own choice, namely, that he offered the gospel without charge. This is something he could determine to do. He would preach the gospel to the Corinthians, at the same time earning his own living, so as not to use to the full his right for maintenance in the gospel.

To summarize the Apostle's argument here, he is making a distinction between what was obligatory and what was optional. There is no thought of any reluctance in his preaching of the gospel. He did that cheerfully. But in a very real sense, it was a solemn obligation that rested upon him. Therefore in the discharge of that obligation there was no reason for his boasting. In preaching the gospel, he could have insisted on his right to financial support, but he did not do this; rather he decided to make the gospel without charge to the Corinthians. Since this was a matter of his own will, he would glory in this. As we have suggested, Paul's critics claimed that his working as a tentmaker indicated that he did not consider himself to be a true apostle. Here he turns his self-support in such a way as to prove that his apostleship was nonetheless real; rather it was of a very high and noble character.

4. Why Paul Waived His Rights (9:19-22)

In verses 19 through 22, Paul cites his example of the waiving of **9:19**

69

legitimate rights for the gospel's sake. In studying this section, it is important to remember that Paul does not mean that he ever sacrificed important principles of the Scripture. He did not believe that the end justified the means. In these verses he is speaking about matters of moral indifference. He accommodated himself to the customs and habits of the people with whom he worked in order that he might gain a ready ear for the gospel. But never did he do anything which might compromise the truth of the gospel.

In one sense he was free from all men. No one could exercise jurisdiction or compulsion over him. Yet he brought himself under bondage to all men in order that he might gain the more. If he could make a concession without sacrificing divine truth he would do it in order to win souls to Christ.

9:20 To the Jews he became as a Jew that he might gain Jews. This cannot mean that he put himself back under the law of Moses in order to see Jews saved. What it does mean might be illustrated in the action which Paul took in connection with the circumcision of Timothy and Titus. In the case of Titus, there were those who insisted that unless he was circumcised, he couldn't be saved. Realizing that this was a frontal attack on the gospel of the grace of God, Paul stoutly refused to have Titus circumcised (Gal. 2:3). However, in the case of Timothy it seems that no such issue was involved. Therefore, the Apostle was willing that Timothy should be circumcised if this would result in a greater hearing of the gospel (Acts 16:3).

In the latter part of verse 20 there is an important change in the New American Standard Bible. It reads, "To those who are under the Law, as under the Law, though *not being myself under the Law,* that I may win those who are under the Law." The words "not being myself under the Law" are not found in the King James Version, but they should be. The expression "those who are under the Law" refers to the Jewish people. But Paul had already spoken of his dealings with the Jews in the first part of the verse. Why does he then repeat the subject here? The explanation that has often been offered is that when he speaks of Jews in the first part of the verse, he is referring to their national customs, whereas here he is referring to their religious life.

At this point a brief word of explanation is necessary. As a Jew, Paul had been born under the law. He sought to obtain favor with God by keeping the law, but found that he was unable to do so. The

70

law only showed him what a wretched sinner he was, and utterly condemned him. Eventually he learned that the law was not a way of salvation, but only God's method of revealing to man his sinfulness and his need of a Savior. Paul then trusted in the Lord Jesus Christ, and in so doing he became free from the condemning voice of the law. The penalty of the law which he had broken was paid by the Lord Jesus Christ on the Cross of Calvary.

After his conversion, the Apostle learned that the law was not the way of salvation, nor was it the rule of life for one who had been saved. The believer is not under law but under grace. This does not mean, of course, that he can go out and do as he pleases. Rather, it means that a true sense of the grace of God will prevent him from even wanting to do these things. Indwelt by the Spirit of God, the Christian is raised to a new level of behavior. He now desires to live a holy life, not out of fear of punishment for having broken the law, but out of love for the Lord Jesus Christ, Who died for him and rose again. Under law the motive was fear, but under grace the motive is love. Love is a far higher motive than fear. Men will do out of love what they would never do from terror.

"God's method of binding souls to obedience is similar to His method of keeping the planets in their orbits—that is, by flinging them out free. You see no chain keeping back these shining worlds to prevent them from bursting away from their center. They are held in the grip of an invisible principle. . . . And it is by the invisible bond of love—love to the Lord who bought them—that ransomed men are constrained to live soberly and righteously and godly"— Arnot.

With that brief background in mind, let us now get back to the latter half of verse 20. "To those who are under the Law, as being under the Law, though not being myself under the Law, that I might win those who are under the Law." When he was with Jewish people, Paul behaved as a Jew in matters of moral indifference. For instance, he ate the foods which the Jewish people ate and refrained from eating such things as pork which were forbidden to them. Perhaps Paul also refrained from working on the Sabbath day, realizing that if he did this, the gospel might gain a more ready hearing from the people.

But notice especially the words "not being myself under the Law." As a born again believer in the Lord Jesus, the Apostle Paul was not under the law as a rule of life. He merely adapted himself to the customs, habits, and prejudices of the people in order that he might win them to the Lord.

9:21   "Paul is not demonstrating two-facedness or multi-facedness, but rather he is testifying of a constant, restrictive self-discipline in order to be able to serve all sorts of men. Just as a narrowly channeled stream is more powerful than an unbounded marshy swamp, so restricted liberty results in more powerful testimony for Christ"— Ryrie.

To those who were without law, Paul acted as one without law, although he himself was not without law to God, but under law to Christ. The expression "them that are without law" does not refer to rebels or criminals who do not recognize any law, but is a general description of Gentile people. The law, as such, was given to the Jewish nation and not to the Gentiles. Thus when Paul was with the Gentiles he complied with their habits and feelings as far as he could possibly do so and still be loyal to the Savior. The Apostle explained that even while he thus acted as without law, he was nevertheless not without law to God. He did not consider that he was free to do as he pleased, but he was under law to Christ. In other words, he was bound to love, honor, serve, and please the Lord Jesus, not now by the law of Moses, but by the law of love. He was "enlawed" to Christ. We have an expression, "When in Rome, do as the Romans do." Paul is saying here that when he was with the Gentiles, he adapted himself to their manner of living as far as he could consistently do so and still be loyal to Christ. But we must keep in mind that this passage deals only with cultural matters and not with doctrinal or moral matters.

9:22   Verse 22 speaks of those who are weak or overscrupulous. They were excessively sensitive about matters that were really not of fundamental importance. To the weak, Paul became weak that he might gain them. He would be a vegetarian if necessary rather than offend them by eating meat. In short, Paul became all things to all men that he might by all means save some. Again we would emphasize that these verses should never be used to justify a sacrifice of Scriptural principle. They merely describe a readiness to accommodate one's self to the customs and habits of the people in order to win a hearing for the good news of salvation. When Paul says "that I may by all means save some," he does not of course think for a moment that he could save another person, for he realized that the Lord Jesus was the

72

only Person who could save. At the same time it is wonderful to notice that those who serve Christ in the gospel are so closely identified with Him that He even allows them to use the word "save" to describe a work in which they are involved. How this exalts and ennobles and dignifies the gospel ministry!

5. Paul's Disciplined Life (9:23-27)

Verses 23 through 27 describe the peril of losing one's reward **9:23** through lack of self-discipline. To Paul the refusal of financial help from the Corinthians was a form of rigid discipline.

In the American Standard Version, verse 23 reads as follows: "And I do all things for the sake of the gospel, that I may become a fellow-partaker of it." In the preceding verses Paul had been describing how he submerged his own rights and desires in the work of the Lord. Why did he do this? He did it for the gospel's sake, in order that he might share in the triumphs of the gospel in a coming day.

Doubtless as the Apostle wrote the words found in verse 24 he **9:24** was reminded of the Isthmian games that were held not far from Corinth. The Corinthian believers would be well-acquainted with those athletic contests. Paul reminds them that while many run in a race, not all receive the prize. The Christian life is like a race. It requires self-discipline. It calls for strenuous effort. It demands definiteness of purpose. The verse does not, however, suggest that in the Christian race only one can win the prize. It simply teaches that we should all run as winners. We should all practice the same kind of self-denial that the Apostle Paul himself practiced. Here, of course, the prize is not salvation, but a reward for faithful service. Salvation is nowhere stated to be the result of our faithfulness in running the race. Salvation is the free gift of God through faith in the Lord Jesus Christ.

In verse 25 the Apostle Paul changes the figure from running to **9:25** wrestling. He reminds his readers that those who strive in the games, that is, those who wrestle, exercise self-control in all things. A wrestler once asked his coach, "Can't I smoke and drink and have a good time and still wrestle?" The coach replied, "Yes, you can do those things, but you can't win."

As Paul thinks of the contestants at the games, he sees the winner stepping up to receive his prize. What is it? It is a corruptible crown, that is, a garland of flowers, or a wreath of leaves that will soon wither and pass away. But in comparison he mentions the incorruptible crown which will be awarded to all those who have been faithful in their service for Christ.

> "We thank Thee for the crown
>   Of glory and of life;
> 'Tis no poor withering wreath of earth,
>   Man's prize in mortal strife;
> 'Tis incorruptible as is the Throne,
>   The Kingdom of our God and His Incarnate Son."

9:26   In view of this incorruptible crown, Paul states that he therefore runs not as uncertainly, and fights not as beating the air. His service was neither purposeless nor ineffectual. He had a definite aim before his eyes, and his intention was that his every action should count. There must be no wasted time or energy. The Apostle was not
9:27   interested in wild misses. Instead, he buffeted his body and brought it into bondage, lest by any means, after he had preached to others, he himself might be rejected or disapproved or be a castaway. If he had catered to the lusts of the flesh, he ran the danger of being a castaway. In the Christian life, there is a necessity for self-control, for temperance, for discipline. We must practice self-mastery.

The Apostle Paul realized the dread possibility that after he had preached to others, he himself might be a castaway. Considerable debate has centered on the meaning of this verse. Some hold that it teaches that a person can be saved and then subsequently lost. This, of course, is in conflict with the general body of teaching in the New Testament to the effect that no true sheep of Christ will ever perish.

Others agree that the word "castaway" is a very strong word and refers to eternal damnation. However, they interpret the verse to mean that Paul is not teaching that a person who was ever saved could be a castaway, but simply that one who failed to exercise self-discipline had never been really saved in the first place. Thinking of the false teachers and how they indulged every passion and appetite, Paul sets forth the general principle that if a person does not keep his body in subjection, this is proof that he never really was born again; and although he might preach to others, he himself will be a castaway.

74

A third explanation is that Paul is not here speaking of salvation at all but of service. He is not suggesting that he might ever be lost, but that he might not stand the test as far as his service was concerned and might be rejected for the prize. We agree with this interpretation. Paul recognizes the awful possibility that, having preached to others, he himself might be put on the shelf by the Lord as no longer usable by Him.

In any event, the passage is an extremely serious one and should cause deep heart-searching on the part of everyone who seeks to serve the Lord Christ. Each one should determine that by the grace of God he will never have to learn the meaning of the passage by experience.

When you have mastered this lesson, take the first part of Exam 3 (covering lesson 5), questions 1-10 on pages 19-22 .

Where to Draw the Line (10:1—11:1)

OUTLINE

VIII. The question of eating meats offered to idols (8:1—11:1). (cont'd).

   E. The history of Israel as an example of the danger of idolatry and self-indulgence (10:1-13).

     1. The privileges of Israel (vv. 1-4).

      a. All under the cloud (v. 1).

      b. All passed through the sea (v. 1).

      c. All baptized unto Moses (v. 2).

      d. All ate the same spiritual food (v. 3).

      e. All drank the same spiritual drink (v. 4).

     2. The punishment of Israel (v. 5).

     3. The causes of Israel's downfall (vv. 6-10).

      a. They lusted after evil things (v. 6).

      b. They committed idolatry (v. 7).

      c. They committed fornication (v. 8).

      d. They tempted the Lord (v. 9).

      e. They murmured (v. 10).

     4. These things happened as examples for us (vv. 11-13).

      a. A warning to the self-confident (vv. 11, 12).

      b. A comfort to the tried (v. 13).

   F. Specific instructions concerning meats offered to idols (10:14—11:1).

     1. Participation in idolatrous feasts at idol temples forbidden (vv. 14-22).

a. Eating at the Lord's Table signifies fellowship with Him (vv. 14:17).
b. Israelites who ate the sacrifices had fellowship with the altar (v. 18).
c. So those who eat at idol feasts are actually fellowshipping with the demons which are associated with the idols (vv. 19, 20).
d. It is morally impossible to fellowship with the Lord and with demons (vv. 21, 22).
    (1) This is to provoke the Lord to jealousy (v. 22).
    (2) It will cause Him to reveal His power in judgment (v. 22).
2. Rules regarding other situations (10:23—11:1).
a. General principles (vv. 23, 24).
    (1) Is it lawful (v. 23)?
    (2) Is it profitable (v. 23)?
    (3) Does it edify (v. 23)?
    (4) Would it be for the welfare of others (v. 24)?
b. Meats sold in the market place may be eaten, even if previously offered to idols (vv. 25, 26).
c. Meats offered to idols may be eaten in a private home unless a weak brother's conscience would be offended (vv. 27-30).
    (1) To cause offense would bring needless condemnation on oneself (vv. 28, 29).
    (2) It would also be the cause of evil-speaking (v. 30).
d. All conduct should be for the glory of God (v. 31), and for the welfare of others (10:1-13)

THE EXAMPLE OF ISRAEL (10:1-13)

1. Israel's Privileges (10:1-4)

As Paul has been thinking of the necessity for self-control, the example of the Israelites comes before his mind. He remembers how they became self-indulgent and careless in the discipline of their bodies, and thus became disqualified, castaway, disapproved.

First of all, he speaks of the privileges of Israel (vv. 1-4); then the punishment of Israel (v. 5); and finally the causes of Israel's downfall (vv. 6-10). Then he explains how these things apply to us (vv. 11-13).

The Apostle reminds the Corinthians that the Jewish fathers were **10:1** all under the cloud and all passed through the sea. In this verse the emphasis is on the word *"all."* He is thinking back to the time of their deliverance from Egypt and of how they were miraculously guided by a pillar of cloud by day and a pillar of fire by night. He is thinking back to the time when they passed through the Red Sea and escaped into the wilderness. As far as privilege was concerned, they all enjoyed divine guidance and divine deliverance.

Not only that, they were all baptized unto Moses in the cloud and **10:2** in the sea. To be baptized unto Moses means to be identified with him and to acknowledge his leadership. As Moses led the children of Israel out of Egypt toward the promised land, all the nation of Israel pledged its allegiance to Moses at first and recognized him as the divinely appointed savior. It has been said that the expression "in the cloud" refers to that which identified them with God, and the expression "in the sea" describes that which separated them from Egypt.

They all ate the same spiritual food. This refers, of course, to the **10:3** manna, which was miraculously provided for the people of Israel as they journeyed through the wilderness. The expression "spiritual food" does not mean that it was non-material. It does not mean that it was invisible or unreal. Rather the expression "spiritual" simply means that the material food was a type or picture of spiritual nourishment, and that the spiritual reality is what the writer had primarily in mind. It may also include the idea that the food was supernaturally given.

All through their journeyings, God wonderfully provided water **10:4** for them to drink. It was real water, but again it is called *spiritual* drink in the sense that it was typical of spiritual refreshment, and miraculously provided. They would have died from thirst many times had not the Lord given them this water in a miraculous way. The expression "they drank of a spiritual Rock that followed them" does not mean that a literal, material rock journeyed behind them as they traveled. The rock signifies the river that flowed from it and that followed the Israelites. The rock was Christ in the sense that He was the One who provided it and the One whom it represents, providing living water to His people.

2. Israel's Punishment (10:5)

10:5 After enumerating all these marvelous privileges that were theirs, the Apostle must now remind the Corinthians that with most of the Israelites God was not well-pleased, for they were overthrown in the wilderness. The King James Version says that with many of them God was not well-pleased. But this is changed in the New American Standard Bible to "with most of them." What the passage is teaching, in simple words, is that although all the nation of Israel left Egypt and all professed to be one in heart and soul with their leader, Moses, yet the sad truth of the matter is that although their bodies were in the wilderness, yet their hearts were still back in Egypt. They enjoyed a physical deliverance from the bondage of Pharaoh, but they still lusted after the sinful pleasures and lusts of that country. We should remind ourselves that of all the warriors over 20 years of age who left Egypt, only two, Caleb and Joshua, ever won the prize, i.e., reached the promised land. The carcasses of the rest of them fell in the wilderness, as an evidence of God's sore displeasure.

The student should recognize the contrast between the word "all" in the first four verses and the word "most" in verse 5. They were all privileged, but most of them perished. "What a sight! The desert strewn with the bodies of such privileged people"—Godet.

3. Israel's Sin (10:6-10)

10:6 In the events that happened back there in the time of the Exodus, we see teaching that applies to us. The children of Israel were actually examples for us, showing us what will happen to us if we also lust after evil things as they did. As we read the Old Testament Scriptures, we should not read them merely as history, but as containing lessons of practical importance for our lives today.

In the verses to follow, the Apostle is going to list some of the specific sins into which they fell. It is worth noticing that many of these sins are concerned with the gratification of bodily appetites.

10:7 Verse 7 refers to the worship of the golden calf and the feast that followed it, as recorded in Exodus 32. When Moses came down from Mount Sinai he found that the people had made a golden calf and were worshiping it. We read in Exodus 32:6 how they sat down to eat and drink and rose up to play, that is, to dance.

10:8 The sin mentioned in verse 8 refers to the time when the sons of

80

Israel intermarried with the daughters of Moab (Num. 25). Seduced by Balaam, the prophet, they disobeyed the Word of the Lord and fell into immorality. We read in verse 8 that there fell in one day twenty-three thousand. In the Old Testament, it is reported that twenty-four thousand died in the plague (Num. 25:9). Critics of the Bible have often used this to show a contradiction in the sacred Scriptures. If they would read the text more carefully, they would see that there is no contradiction. In 1 Corinthians 10, verse 8, it simply states that twenty-three thousand fell *in one day*. In the Old Testament, the figure of twenty-four thousand describes the entire number that died *in the plague*.

10:9 Paul next alludes to the time when the children of Israel expressed dissatisfaction with the food and expressed doubt as to the goodness of the Lord. At that time God sent serpents among them and many perished (Num. 21:5, 6). Here again it is noticeable how food gratification was their downfall.

10:10 The sin of Korah, Dathan, and Abiram is referred to here (Num. 16:14-47). Again there was murmuring against the Lord because of the food situation (Num. 16:14). The Israelites did not practice self-control with regard to their bodies. They did not buffet their bodies and put them in a place of subjection. Rather, they made provision for the lusts of the flesh, and this proved to be their downfall.

10:11 The next three verses give the practical application of the lessons that have been before us. First of all, in this verse, Paul explains that the meaning of these events is not limited to their historical value. They have a significance for us today. They were written as a warning to us who are living after the close of the Jewish age and during the gospel age, "to us to whom the revenues of the past ages have descended"—Dr. Rendall Harris. They constitute a warning to the 10:12 self-confident. "Let him that thinketh he standeth take heed lest he fall." Perhaps this refers especially to the strong believer who thinks he can dabble with self-gratification and not be affected by it. Such a person is in greatest danger of falling under the disciplinary hand of God.

10:13 But then Paul would add a word of comfort for those who are tried. The Apostle teaches that the testings and trials and temptations which face us are common to all men. However, our faithful God will not allow us to be tested above what we are able. He does not promise to deliver us from temptation or testing, but He does

81

promise to limit it in its intensity. He further promises to provide a way of escape, that we may be able to bear it. As one reads this verse, he cannot help but be struck by the tremendous comfort it has afforded to tested saints of God down through the centuries. Young believers have clung to it as to a life-line and older believers have reposed on it as upon a pillow. Perhaps some of Paul's readers were being fiercely tempted at the time to go into idolatry. Paul would comfort them with the thought that God would not allow any unbearable temptation to come into their way. At the same time they should be warned that they should not expose themselves to temptation.

THINGS WE MUST NOT DO (10:14-22)

10:14 The section from verse 14 through the first verse of the next chapter returns to deal more specifically with the subject of meats offered to idols. First of all, Paul takes up the question as to whether believers should participate in feasts in idol temples (vv. 14-22).

"Wherefore, my dearly beloved, flee from idolatry." Perhaps it was a real test for the believers at Corinth to be invited to participate in an idol feast at one of the temples. Some might feel that they were above temptation. Perhaps they would say that surely it would not hurt to go just once. The Apostle's inspired advice is to flee from idolatry. He does not say to study about it, to become better acquainted with it, or to trifle with it in any way. To flee is to run in the opposite direction.

10:15 Paul knows that he is addressing himself to intelligent men—to men who can understand what he is saying.

10:16 In verse 16 Paul makes reference to the Lord's Supper. He says first of all, "Is not the cup of blessing which we bless, a sharing in the blood of Christ?" (NASB). The "cup of blessing" refers to the cup of wine which is used at the Lord's Supper. It is a cup which speaks of the tremendous blessing which has come to us through the death of Christ; therefore it is called the cup of blessing. The clause "which we bless" means "for which we give thanks." When we take that cup and press it to our lips, we are saying in effect that we are participants in all the benefits that flow from the blood of Christ. Therefore we might paraphrase this verse as follows: "The cup which speaks of the tremendous blessings which have come to us through the blood of the Lord Jesus, and the same cup for which we give thanks, what is it but a testimony to the fact that all believers are partakers of the benefits of the blood of Christ?"

The same thing is true of the bread which we break, the communion loaf. As we eat the bread, we say, in effect, that we have all been saved through the offering of His body on the Cross of Calvary and that we are therefore members of His body. In short, the cup and the loaf speak of fellowship with Christ, of participating in His glorious ministry for us.

The question has been raised of why the blood should be mentioned first in this verse whereas in the institution of the Lord's Supper, the bread is mentioned first. A possible answer is that Paul is here speaking of the order of events when we come into the Christian fellowship. Usually a new convert understands the value of the blood of Christ before he recognizes the truth of the one body. Thus this verse might give the order in which we understand salvation.

All believers, though many, are one body in Christ, represented by **10:17** the loaf of bread. All partake of the one bread in the sense that all have fellowship in the benefits that flow from the giving of the body of Christ.

What Paul is saying in these verses is that eating at the Lord's Table **10:18** signifies fellowship with Him. The same was true of those Israelites who ate the sacrifices. It meant that they had fellowship with the altar. The reference here, no doubt, is to the peace offering. The people brought their sacrifices to the temple. A portion of the offering was burnt on the altar with fire; another portion was reserved for the priests; and the third part was set aside for the offerer and his friends. They ate of the offering on the same day. Paul is emphasizing that all who ate of the offering identified themselves with God and with the nation of Israel and, in short, with all of which the altar spoke.

But how does all this fit in with the portion of Scripture that we are **10:19** studying? The answer is quite simple. Just as partaking of the Lord's Supper speaks of fellowship with the Lord, and just as the Israelites partaking of the peace offering spoke of fellowship with the altar of Jehovah, so eating at an idol feast in the temple speaks of fellowship with the idols.

"What do I mean then? That a thing sacrificed to idols is anything, or that an idol is anything?" (N.A.S.B). Does Paul mean to imply by all of this that meat that has been offered to idols changes its character or quality? Or does he mean to say that an idol is real, that it hears, sees, and has power? The answer to both of these questions is, **10:20** of course, in the negative. What Paul does want to emphasize is that the things that the Gentiles offer are offered to demons. In some strange and mysterious way, idol worship is linked with demons. Using the idols, the demons control the hearts and minds of those who worship them.

10:21 In the King James Version the word "devils" in verse 20 should be translated "demons." There is one devil, that is Satan, but there are many demons that are his messengers and agents. Paul adds, "And I do not want you to become sharers in demons" (N.A.S.B).

In the New American Standard Bible, verse 21 reads: *"You cannot drink the cup of the Lord, and the cup of demons: you cannot partake of the table of the Lord, and the table of demons."* The cup of the Lord in this verse is a figurative expression to describe the benefits which come to us through Christ. It is a figure of speech known as metonymy, where the container is used to denote the things contained. The expression "the table of the Lord" is likewise a figurative expression. It is not the same as the Lord's Supper, although it might include the latter. A table is an article of furniture where food is set out and where fellowship is enjoyed. Here the Table of the Lord means the sum total of the blessings which we enjoy in Christ.

When Paul says that you cannot drink the cup of the Lord and the cup of demons, that you cannot partake of the Table of the Lord and of the table of demons, he does not mean that it is a physical impossibility. It would be a physical possibility, for instance, for a believer to go to an idol temple and to participate in a feast there. But what Paul means here is that it would be morally inconsistent. It would be an act of treachery and disloyalty to the Lord Jesus to profess adherence or allegiance to Him, on the one hand, and then to go and have fellowship with those who sacrifice to idols. It would be morally improper and utterly wrong.

10:22 Not only that, it would not be possible to do this without provoking the Lord to jealousy. As William Kelly has said, "Love cannot but be jealous of wandering affections; it would not be love if it did not resent unfaithfulness." The Christian should fear to thus displease the Lord, or to provoke His righteous indignation. Do we think that we are stronger than He? That is, do we dare thus to grieve Him and

84

to risk an exhibition of His disciplinary judgment upon us?

THINGS WE MAY DO WITH CARE (10:23—11:1)

The Apostle turns from the subject of participation in idol feasts and **10:23** takes up some general principles that should govern Christians in their daily life. When he says *"all things are lawful,"* he does not mean all things in an absolute sense. For instance, he is not implying for a moment that it would be lawful for him to commit murder or to get drunk. Here again we must understand the expression as referring only to matters of moral indifference. There is a great area in Christian life where things are perfectly legitimate in themselves and yet where for other reasons it would not be wise for a Christian to participate. Thus Paul says, "All things are lawful, but not all things are profitable" (N.A.S.B.). For instance, a thing might be quite lawful for a believer and yet might be equally unwise in view of the national customs of the people where he dwells. Also things that are lawful in themselves might not be edifying. That is, a thing might not result in building up a brother in his most holy faith. Should I then be high-handed in demanding my own rights or should I consider what would help my brother in Christ?

In verses 23-30, some of the modern versions (RSV, TEV, NEB) indicate by quotation marks where they understand the Apostle is quoting the Corinthians and where he is replying to them.

In all the decisions which we make, we should not be selfishly **10:24** thinking of what will benefit ourselves, but we should rather think what would be for our neighbor's wealth, i.e., his welfare or benefit. The principles we are studying in this section could very well be applied to matters of dress, of entertainment, of food and drink, of one's standard of living, of the entertainments in which he participates.

The shambles in verse 25 refer to the market place. If a believer **10:25** went to the butcher shop to purchase some meat, he was not required to ask the merchant whether that meat had been previously offered to idols. The meat itself would not be affected in one way or another, and there would be no question of loyalty to Christ involved. In explanation of this advice, Paul quotes from Psalm 24:1: **10:26** "The earth is the Lord's, and the fulness thereof." The thought here is that the food that we eat has been graciously provided by the Lord

85

for us and is specifically intended for our use. Heinrici tells us that these words from Psalm 24 are commonly used among the Jews as a thanksgiving at the table.

10:27 In verse 27 Paul takes up another situation which might cause the believers to ask questions. Supposing a man should invite a believer to his home for a meal. Let us say that the host is not a believer. Would a Christian be free to accept such an invitation? The answer is yes. If you are invited to a meal in an unbeliever's home and you are disposed to go, you are at liberty to eat what is set before you, asking
10:28 no question for conscience' sake. If, during the course of a meal, another Christian should be present who has a weak conscience and he informs you that the meat you are eating has been offered to idols, should you then go on and eat it? The answer is that you should not indulge because in so doing you might be stumbling him and hurting his conscience. Neither should you eat if an unbeliever would be hindered in accepting the Lord through this action.

The student should notice that the expression "for the earth is the Lord's, and the fulness thereof" at the end of verse 28 is not part of the original, and should be omitted. It obviously does not make good sense in this verse, whereas it is very meaningful in verse 26.

10:29 The meaning of verse 29 seems to be this: in the case just cited you would not refrain from eating because of your own conscience. You would have perfect liberty, as a believer, to eat the meat. But the weak brother sitting by has a conscience about it, and so you refrain from eating out of respect to his conscience and not because your own conscience condemns the act.

The question "For why is my liberty judged by another man's conscience?" could perhaps be paraphrased as follows: "Why should I selfishly display my liberty to eat the meat and in so doing be condemned by the other man's conscience? Why should I expose my liberty to the condemnation of his conscience? Why should I let my good be evil spoken of?" (see Rom. 14:16). Is a piece of meat so important that I should cause such an offense to a fellow-believer in the Lord Jesus Christ? However, in all fairness, it should be added that many commentators believe that Paul is here quoting the objection of the Corinthians, or asking a rhetorical question, before answering in the following verses.

10:30 It seems that the Authorized Version of verse 30 gives a wrong impression. According to this translation, Paul seems to be standing up for his rights. He seems to imply that as long as he gives thanks for food, he has a right to eat it, no matter what any one else would say. But that is the exact opposite of what the Apostle is teaching in this whole section. What the Apostle seems to be saying is that to him it seems very contradictory to give thanks to God on the one hand, when by so doing he is wounding a brother.

The expression "for if I by grace be a partaker" means "if I partake with thankfulness." The argument is this: it is better to deny one's self a legitimate right than to give thanks to God for something which will cause others to speak evil of you. William Kelly comments that it is "better to deny one's self and not allow one's liberty to be condemned by another or incur evil speaking for that for which one gives thanks." Why make such a use of liberty as to give offense? Why let my giving of thanks be exposed to misconstruction or be called sacrilege or scandal?

There are two great rules to guide us in all our Christian lives. The **10:31** first is the glory of God, and the second is the welfare of our fellow men. Paul gives the first of these in verse 31: "Whether therefore ye eat, or drink, or whatsoever ye do, do all to the glory of God." Christian young people are often faced with decisions as to whether a certain course of action would be right or wrong for them. Here is a good rule to apply: Is there any glory for God in it? Can you bow your head before you participate in it and ask the Lord that He will be greatly magnified by what you are about to do?

The second rule is the welfare of our fellow men. We should do **10:32** nothing that would give offense or that would give an occasion of stumbling, either to the Jews or to the Greeks or to the Church of God. Here Paul divides all mankind into three classes. The Jews, of course, are the nation of Israel. The Greeks are the unconverted Gentiles, whereas the Church of God includes all true believers in the Lord Jesus Christ. In one sense we are bound to offend others and excite their wrath if we faithfully witness to them. However, that is not what is spoken of here. Rather, the Apostle is thinking here of needless offense. He is cautioning us against using our legitimate rights in such a way as to stumble others. Paul can honestly say that **10:33** he seeks to please all men in all things, not seeking his own good, but the good of the many. Probably few men have ever lived so unselfishly for others as the great Apostle Paul.

Verse 1 of chapter 11 probably belongs with the previous chapter. **11:1**

87

Paul had just been speaking of how he tried to gauge all his actions in the light of their effect on others. Now he tells the Corinthians to be imitators of him, even as he also is of Christ. He renounced personal advantages and rights in order to help those about him. The Corinthians should do likewise, and not selfishly parade their liberties in such a way as to hinder the gospel of Christ or offend the weak brother.

When you are ready, complete Exam 3 by answering questions 11-20 on pages 22-24. (You should have already answered questions 1-10 as part of your study of Lesson 5.)

Questions About Women and Worship (11:2-34)

OUTLINE

IX. Instructions concerning woman's head-covering (11:2-16).
   A. Preliminary word of commendation (v. 2).
   B. The spheres of headship in the universe (v. 3).
      1. Christ is head of man.
      2. Man is head of woman.
      3. God is head of Christ.
   C. Man should pray or prophesy with head uncovered, but woman should be covered when praying or prophesying (vv. 4-16).
      1. Otherwise she dishonors her head (vv. 4, 5).
      2. To be uncovered is shameful (v. 6).
      3. The facts of creation teach the subordination of woman to man (vv. 7-10).
         a. Man is the glory of God; woman the glory of the man (v. 7).
         b. Woman was created from man (v. 8).
         c. Woman was created for man (v. 9).
         d. Woman should therefore wear a symbol of her subjection (v. 10).
      4. Man and woman are mutually dependent on each other, and the position of each is by divine appointment (vv. 11, 12).
      5. Nature teaches that women should be covered (vv. 13-15).

a. It is a shame for a man to have long hair (v. 14).

b. It is a glory for a woman to have long hair (v. 15).

6. The custom of the apostles and of the churches was for the women to be covered (v. 16).

X. Abuses in connection with the Lord's Supper (11:17-34).

A. Rebuke for divisions among them as they gathered together (vv. 17-19).

B. Rebuke for confusing the Lord's Supper with a common meal (vv. 20-22).

C. The origin and intent of the Lord's Supper (vv. 23-26).

D. The consequences of participating unworthily (vv. 27-32).

E. Admonition to consider others and to avoid punishment (vv. 33, 34).

THE WOMAN'S HEAD COVERING (11:2-16)

From verse 2 through verse 16 of this chapter, we have a section devoted to the subject of woman's head-covering. The remaining verses deal with abuses in connection with the Lord's Supper (vv. 17-34). The first section of the chapter has been a much disputed portion of Paul's letter to the Corinthians. Some think that the instruction given here was applicable only to the day in which Paul lived. Some go so far as to contend that these verses reflect Paul's personal prejudice against women, since he was a bachelor. Still others accept the teaching of this portion in a simple manner, seeking to obey its precepts even if they do not understand them all.

11:2 The Apostle first of all commends the Corinthians for the way in which they remembered him in all things, and held fast the traditions, as he had delivered them to them. The word "ordinances" in the King James Version should be translated "traditions," and it refers not to habits and practices that have arisen in the church down through the years, but rather in this case, to the inspired instructions of the Apostle Paul.

1. The Matter of Headship (11:3-12)

11:3 Paul now introduces the subject of women's covering. Behind his instruction is the fact that every ordered society is built on two pillars—authority and subjection to that authority. It is impossible to have a well-functioning community where these two principles are not observed. Paul mentions three great relationships involving authority and subjection. First, the head of every man is Christ; Christ is Lord and man is subject to Him. Secondly, the head of the woman is the man; the place of headship was given to the man, and the woman is under his authority. Third, the head of Christ is God; even in the Godhead, One Person has the place of rule and Another takes the place of willing subordination. These examples of headship and submission were designed by God Himself and are fundamental in His arrangement of the universe.

At the outset it should be emphasized that subjection does not mean inferiority. Christ is subject to God the Father but He is not inferior to Him. Neither is the woman inferior to the man though she is subordinate to him.

For a man to pray or prophesy with his head covered is to dishonor **11:4** his Head, i.e., Christ. It is saying, in effect, that the man does not acknowledge Christ as his head. Thus it is an act of gross disrespect.

If a woman prays or prophesies with her head uncovered, she **11:5** dishonors her head, i.e., the man. She is saying, in effect, that she does recognize man's God-given headship and will not submit to it.

If this were the only verse in the Bible on the subject, then it would imply that it is all right for a woman to pray or prophesy in the assembly as long as she has a veil or other covering on her head. But Paul elsewhere teaches that women should be silent in the assembly (1 Cor. 14:34), that they are not permitted to teach or to usurp authority over the man but to be in silence (1 Tim. 2:12).

The passage is admittedly a difficult one. What does seem clear is that in the matter of covering, the woman's duty is the exact opposite of the man's. In other words, it is proper for a woman to be covered whenever it is proper for a man to be uncovered in situations involving prayer and prophesying.

If a woman is not veiled, she might as well be shorn, but if it is a **11:6** shame for a woman to be shorn, then she should be veiled. The unveiled head of a woman is as shameful as if her hair were cut off. The Apostle is not commanding a barbering operation but rather telling what moral consistency would require.

In verses 7-10, Paul teaches the subordination of woman to man **11:7** by going back to creation. This should forever lay to rest any idea that his teaching about woman's covering was what was culturally suitable in his day but not applicable to us today. The headship of man and the subjection of woman have been God's order from the very beginning.

First of all, man is the glory of God whereas woman is the glory of the man. This means that man was placed on earth as God's representative, to exercise dominion over it. Man's uncovered head is a silent witness to this fact. Woman was never given this place of headship; instead she is the glory of the man in the sense that she "renders conspicuous the authority of man"—W. E. Vine.

Man ought not to cover his head; it would be tantamount to veiling the glory of God, and this would be an insult to the Divine Majesty.

11:8 Paul next reminds us that man was not created from the woman but that the woman was created from the man. The man was first, then the woman was taken from his side. This priority of the man strengthens the Apostle's case for man's headship.

11:9 The purpose of creation is next alluded to in order to press home the point. Man was not created primarily for the woman, but rather the woman for the man. The Lord distinctly stated in Genesis 2:18, "It is not good that the man should be alone; I will make him an help meet for him."

11:10 Because of her position of subordination to the man, the woman ought "to have power on her head because of the angels." This is a very obscure statement, as it stands in the Authorized Version. We believe that it means that a woman should have a symbol of power or authority on her head because of the angels. The symbol of power or authority is the head-covering and it indicates not her own authority but her subjection to the authority of her husband.

But then why does it add "because of the angels"? We would suggest that the angels are spectators of the things that are happening in the church, as they were of the things that happened at creation. In the first creation, they saw that woman usurped the place of headship over the man. She made the decision that Adam should have made. As a result of this, sin entered the human race with its unspeakable aftermath of misery and woe. God does not want what happened in the first creation to be repeated in the new creation. When the angels look down upon the church, He wants them to see the woman acting in subjection to the man, and indicating this outwardly by a covering on her head.

We might pause here to state that the head covering is simply an outward sign and it is only of value when it is the outward sign of an inward grace. In other words, a woman might have a covering on her head and yet not truly be in subjection to her husband. In such a case, to wear a head-covering would be of no value at all. The most important thing is to be sure that the heart is truly subordinate; then a covering on a woman's head becomes truly meaningful.

Paul would not want anything that he has said to be understood as 11:11 implying that man is at all independent of the woman. Therefore he adds, "Nevertheless, neither is the man without the woman, neither the woman without the man, in the Lord." In other words, man and woman are mutually dependent upon each other. They need one another and the idea of subordination is not at all in conflict with the idea of mutual interdependence. The woman is of the man by cre- 11:12 ation, that is, she was created from the man. But Paul points out that the man is also by the woman. Here he is referring to the process of birth. The woman gives birth to the man child. Thus God has created this perfect balance to indicate that the one cannot exist without the other.

Then Paul adds that all things are of God, that is, it is God who has divinely appointed all these things, so there is no just cause for complaint. Not only were these relationships created by God, but the purpose of them all is to glorify Him. All of this should make the man humble and the woman content.

2. The Covering (11:13-15)

The Apostle now challenges the Corinthians to judge in themselves 11:13 if it is comely for a woman to pray to God unveiled. He appeals to their instinctive sense. The suggestion is that it is not reverent or decorous for a woman to enter into the presence of God unveiled.

Just how nature teaches us that it is a shame for a man to have long 11:14 hair is not made clear. Some have suggested that a man's hair will not naturally grow into long tresses as a woman's will do. For a man to have long hair makes him appear effeminate. The occurrence of baldness among men has also been mentioned in this connection, an occurrence which while not completely unknown among women is nevertheless quite uncommon.

Verse 15 has been greatly misunderstood by students of the Bible. 11:15 Many have suggested that since a woman's hair is given to her for a covering, it is not necessary for her to have any other covering. But such a teaching does grave violence to this portion of Scripture. Unless the student sees that two coverings are mentioned in this chapter, then the passage becomes hopelessly confused. This may be demonstrated by referring back to verse 6. There we read: "For if a woman is not veiled, let her also be shorn." According to the interpretation just mentioned, this would mean that if a woman does not have her hair on, then she might just as well be shorn. But this would be ridiculous. If she did not have her hair on, there would be no need for her to be shorn.

The actual argument in verse 15 is that there is a real analogy between the spiritual and the natural. God gave woman a natural covering of glory in a way He did not give to man. There is a spiritual significance to this. It teaches that when a woman prays to God, she should wear a veil over her head. What is true in the natural sphere should be true in the spiritual.

11:16   The Apostle closes this section with the statement, "If any man seem to be contentious, we have no such custom, neither the churches of God." What does Paul mean by this statement? Does he mean, as has been suggested, that the things he has just been saying are not important enough to contend about? Does he mean that there was no such custom of woman veiling their heads in the churches of God? Does he mean that these teachings are optional and not to be pressed upon women as the commandments of the Lord? It seems strange that any such interpretations would ever be offered, yet they are commonly heard today. This would mean that Paul considered these instructions as of no real consequence, and he had just been wasting his time in setting them forth.

There are at least two possible explanations of this verse, explanations which fit in with the rest of the Scripture. First of all, the Apostle Paul may be saying that he anticipates that certain ones will be contentious about these matters, but he adds that we have no such custom, that is, the custom of contending about this. We do not argue about such matters, but accept them as the teachings of the Lord. Another interpretation is that Paul was saying that the churches of God did not have any such custom as that of women attending public services without being covered. William Kelly favors this latter view.

94

THE LORD'S SUPPER (11:17-34)

1. Divisions and Disorders (11:17-22)

The Apostle rebukes the Corinthians for the fact that there were 11:17 divisions among them as they gathered together (vv. 17-19). Note the repetition of the expression "when ye come together" or related words (11:17, 18, 20, 33, 34; 14:23, 26). In verse 2 of this chapter Paul had had occasion to praise them for keeping the traditions which he had delivered to them, but there was one matter in which he could not praise them, and that is the matter about which he is to speak. When they gathered together for public meetings, they came together not for the better, but for the worse. This is a solemn reminder to us all that it is possible to go away from meetings of the church and to have been harmed rather than benefited.

The first cause of rebuke was the existence of divisions or schisms. 11:18 This does not mean that parties had broken away from the church and formed separate fellowships, but rather that there were cliques and factions within the local church. A schism is a party within, whereas a sect is a different party without. Paul could believe these reports of divisions because he knew that the Corinthians were in a carnal state, and he had previous occasion in this epistle to rebuke them because of their divisions.

"Paul was prepared to give at least partial credence to the reports of the divisions at Corinth, since he knew that, owing to their carnal state, there were bound to be these opinionated factions in their midst. Here Paul reasons forward from their state to their actions. Knowing them to be carnal and walking as men, he knew that they would certainly fall victims to the inveterate tendency of the human mind to form its strong opinions, and the factions founded in those opinions, ending in the schisms and divisions. He knew, too, that God could overrule their folly and take occasion to make manifest those that were approved of Him, walking according to the Spirit and not as man; and consequently eschewing the whole of this divisive business"—F. B. Hole.

Paul foresaw that the schisms already begun in Corinth would 11:19 increase until they became of a more serious nature. Although in general this would be detrimental to the church, yet one good thing would come out of it, that is, that those who were truly spiritual men, and who were approved of God, would be manifest to the Corinthians. When Paul says in this verse, "there must be also heresies among you," this does not mean that it is a moral necessity. God is not here condoning heresies. Rather Paul means that because of the carnal conditions of the Corinthians, it was inevitable that heresies should result. Heresies here, incidentally, do not refer to unorthodox teachings, as the word means today, but rather to serious splits in the church. Divisions are a proof that some have failed to discern the mind of the Lord.

11:20   Paul now directs his second rebuke against abuses in connection with the Lord's Supper. When the Christians gathered together, ostensibly to celebrate the Lord's Supper, their conduct was of such a deplorable nature that Paul says they would not possibly remember the Lord in the way in which He appointed. They might go through the outward motions, but their entire deportment would preclude any true remembrance of the Lord.

11:21   In the early days of the Church, the Christians celebrated the "agape," or love feast, and also the Lord's Supper. The love feast was something like a common meal, partaken in a spirit of love and fellowship. At the end of the love feast, the Christians often had the remembrance of the Lord with the bread and the wine. But before very long, abuses crept in. For instance, in this verse it is implied that the love feast lost its real meaning. Not only did the Christians not wait for one another, but the rich ones shamed their poorer brethren by having lavish meals and not sharing them. Some went away hungry, whereas others were actually drunken. Since the Lord's Supper sometimes followed the love feast, they would still be drunk when they sat down to partake of the Lord's Supper.

11:22   The Apostle indignantly rebukes such disgraceful conduct. If they insist in carrying on in such a way, then they should at least have the reverence not to do so in the local church. To practice intemperance at a time when the church of God is gathered together, and to shame one's poorer brethren, is most inconsistent with the Christian profession. Paul cannot but withhold praise from the saints for acting in this way; and in withholding praise, he thereby condemns them strongly.

2. The Origin and Purpose of the Lord's Supper (11:23-26)

11:23 To show the contrast between their conduct and the real meaning of the Lord's Supper, he goes back to its original institution. He shows that it was not a common meal or a feast, but a solemn ordinance of the Lord. Paul received his knowledge concerning this directly from the Lord and he mentions this to show that any violation would be actual disobedience. What he is teaching, then, he received by revelation.[1]

First of all, he mentions how that the Lord Jesus took bread on the very night in which He was betrayed. The literal meaning is "while He was being betrayed." While the foul plot to deliver Him up was going on outside, the Lord Jesus gathered in the upper room with His disciples and took the bread.

The fact that this occurred at night does not necessarily mean that the Lord's Supper must thereafter be observed only at night. At that time, sundown was the beginning of the Jewish day. Our day begins at sunrise. Also it has been remarked that there is a difference between apostolic example and apostolic precept. We are not obligated to do all that the apostles did, but we are most certainly obligated to obey all that they taught.

The Lord Jesus took the bread, first of all, and gave thanks for it. **11:24** Since the bread was typical of His body, He was, in effect, thanking God that He had been given a human body in which He might come and die for the sins of the world.

When the Savior said, "This is my body," did He mean that the bread actually became His body in some real sense? The Roman Catholic teaching of transubstantiation insists that the bread and the wine are literally changed into the body and the blood of Christ. The Lutheran doctrine of consubstantiation teaches that the true body and blood of Christ are in, with, and under the bread and wine on the table.

In answer to these views, it should be sufficient to remind the student that when the Lord Jesus instituted this memorial, His body had not yet been given, nor had His blood been shed. When the Lord Jesus said, "This is my body," He meant, "This is symbolic of my body" or "This is a picture of my body which is given for you." To eat the bread is to remember Him in His atoning death for us. "There is ineffable tenderness in the expression of Jesus 'in remembrance of me' "—Godet.

[1]Students interested in studying the subject of the Lord's Supper in greater detail should enroll in the Emmaus course *The Lord's Supper*.

11:25 In like manner the Lord Jesus took the cup after the Passover supper, saying, "This cup is the new covenant in My blood; do this, as often as you drink it, in remembrance of Me" (N.A.S.B). The Lord's Supper was instituted immediately after the Passover feast. That is why it says that the Lord Jesus took the cup *when He had supped.* In connection with the cup, He said that it was the new testament in His blood. The new testament is the same as the new covenant. This refers to the covenant that God promised to the nation of Israel in Jeremiah 31:31-34. It is an unconditional promise by which He agreed to be merciful to their unrighteousness and to remember their sins and iniquities no more. The terms of the new covenant are also given in Hebrews 8:10-12. The covenant is in force at the present time, but unbelief keeps the nation of Israel from enjoying it. All who do trust the Lord Jesus receive the benefits that were promised. When the people of Israel turn to the Lord, they will enjoy the blessings of the new covenant; that will be during Christ's thousand-year reign on earth. This new covenant was ratified by the blood of Christ, and that is why He speaks of the cup as being the new testament in His blood. It means "the new testament ratified by My Blood." The foundation of the new covenant was laid through the Cross.

11:26 Verse 26 touches the question as to how frequently the Lord's Supper should be observed. "As often as ye eat . . . and drink . . ." No legalistic rule is laid down; neither is any fixed date given. It seems clear from Acts 20:7 that the practice of the disciples was to meet on the first day of the week to remember the Lord. That this ordinance was not intended simply for the early days of the Church is abundantly proved by the expression "till He come." Godet beautifully points out that the Lord's Supper is "the link between His two comings, the monument of the one, the pledge of the other."

In all this instruction concerning the Lord's Supper it is noticeable that there is no word about a minister officiating. It is a simple memorial service left for all the people of God. Christians gather together simply as believer-priests to thus proclaim the Lord's death till He comes.

3. Warnings (11:27-34)

11:27 Having discussed the origin and purpose of the Lord's Supper, the

Apostle now turns to the consequences of participating in it unworthily. Whoever eats the bread or drinks the cup of the Lord in an unworthy manner is guilty of the body and the blood of the Lord. In one sense, we are all unworthy to partake of this solemn Supper. In that sense, we are unworthy of any of the Lord's mercy or kindness to us. But that is not the subject here. The Apostle is not speaking of our own personal unworthiness. Cleansed by the blood of Christ, we can approach God in all the worthiness of His own beloved Son. But Paul is here speaking of the disgraceful conduct which characterized the Corinthians as they gathered together for the Lord's Supper. They were guilty of careless, irreverent behavior. To act thus is to be guilty of the body and the blood of the Lord.

As we come to the Lord's Supper, we should do so in a judged 11:28 condition. Sin should be confessed and forsaken; restitution should be made; apologies should be offered to those whom we have offended. In general we should make sure that we are in a proper state of soul. To eat and to drink in an inconsistent manner is to eat and 11:29 drink judgment to one's self, not discerning the Lord's body. We should realize that the Lord's body was given in order that our sins might be put away. If we go on living in sin, while at the same time partaking of the Lord's Supper, we are living a lie. "If we eat the Lord's Supper with unjudged sin upon us, we do not discern the Lord's body which was broken to put it away"—F. G. Patterson.

Failure to exercise self-judgment resulted in God's disciplinary 11:30 judgment upon some in the church in Corinth. Some were weak and sickly and not a few slept. In other words, physical illness had come upon some, and some were taken home to heaven. In the damnation or judgment spoken of in these verses, there is no thought of eternal death. The Apostle is speaking of believers in this passage and stating simply that because they did not judge sin in their lives, the Lord was required to take disciplinary action against them. On the other hand, 11:31 if we exercise this self-judgment, it will not be necessary to so chasten us.

God is dealing with us as with His own children. He loves us too 11:32 dearly to allow us to go on in sin. Thus we soon feel the shepherd's crook on our necks pulling us back to Himself. As someone has said, "It is possible for the saints to be fit for heaven (in Christ) but not fitted to remain on the earth in testimony."

When the believers come together for the love feast, or agape, 11:33

99

they should wait for one another, and not selfishly proceed without regard for the other saints. "Waiting for one another" is in contrast to 11:34 verse 21, "everyone taketh before another his own supper." If any man is hungry, he should eat at home. In other words, the love feast, linked as it was then with the Lord's Supper, was not to be mistaken for a common meal. To disregard its sacred character would be to come together unto judgment.

"And the rest will I set in order when I come." Undoubtedly there were other matters of minor importance which had been mentioned to the Apostle Paul in the letter from the Corinthians. Here he assures them that he will deal with these matters personally when he visits them.

When you have mastered this lesson, take the first part of Exam 4 (covering lesson 7), questions 1-10 on pages 25-27.

Lesson 8

The Gifts of the Spirit (12:1-20)

OUTLINE

XI. The gifts of the Spirit and their use in the Church (chapters 12-14).
  A. Christians should not be ignorant of spirit manifestations (12:1, 2).
  B. The test of true testimony of the Holy Spirit—the confession that Jesus is Lord (v. 3).
  C. The variety of gifts, yet their threefold unity (vv. 4-6).
    1. All directed by the same Spirit (v. 4).
    2. All serve the same Lord (v. 5).
    3. All originate with the same God (v. 6).
  D. The common purpose of the gifts—to benefit the whole church (v. 7).
  E. The names of some of the gifts of the Spirit (vv. 8-10).
  F. The Spirit distributes these gifts sovereignly as He pleases (v. 11).
  G. The unity and diversity of the Spirit's work illustrated by the human body (vv. 12-31).
    1. One body yet many members is true of the human body and of the Church (v. 12).
    2. All believers were baptized into the body of Christ and all partake of the same Spirit (v. 13).
    3. The folly of discontent among members of the body (vv. 14-20).
      a. Any body requires many members (v. 14).
      b. Envy of other members is ridiculous (vv. 15, 16).

c. Every member has a distinct function (v. 17).

d. It is God who has assigned these function (v. 18).

e. With only one member, there would be no body, but with many members, there is one body (vv. 19, 20).

GIFTS AND THE SPIRIT (12:1-3)

Chapters 12 through 14 deal with the gifts of the Spirit. There had been abuses in the assembly in Corinth, especially in connection with the gift of tongues, and Paul writes in order to correct those abuses.

There were believers in Corinth who had received the gift of tongues, which means that they were given the power to speak foreign languages without ever having studied those languages. But instead of using this gift to magnify God and to edify the other believers, they were using it to show off. They stood up in the meetings and spoke in languages which no one else understood, hoping that the others would be impressed by their linguistic proficiency. They exalted the sign-gifts above the others, and claimed superior spirituality for those who spoke in tongues. This led to pride on the one hand, and to feelings of envy, inferiority and worthlessness on the other. It was therefore necessary for the Apostle to correct these erroneous attitudes and to establish controls in the exercise of the gifts, especially tongues and prophecy.

12:1 He does not want the saints at Corinth to be ignorant in the matter of spiritual manifestations or gifts. The literal reading here is "Now concerning spirituals, brethren, I would not have you ignorant." Most versions supply the word "gifts" to complete the sense. However, the next verse suggests that Paul might have been thinking not only of manifestations of the Holy Spirit but of evil spirits as well.

12:2 Before conversion the Corinthians had been idolaters, enslaved by evil spirits. They lived in fear of the spirits and were led about by these diabolical influences. They witnessed supernatural manifestations of the spirit world and heard spirit-inspired utterances. Under the influence of evil spirits, they sometimes surrendered self-control, and said and did things beyond their own conscious powers.

12:3 Now that they are saved, the believers must know how to judge all spirit-manifestations, that is, how to discern between the voice of evil spirits and the authentic voice of the Holy Spirit. The crucial test is

102

the testimony that is given concerning the Lord Jesus. If a man says, "Jesus is accursed," you can be sure that he is demon-inspired, because evil spirits characteristically blaspheme and curse the name of Jesus. The Holy Spirit would never lead anyone to speak of the Savior in this way; His ministry is to exalt the Lord Jesus. He leads people to say "Jesus is Lord," not just to say it with their lips, but with the warm, full confession of their hearts.

Notice that the three Persons of the Trinity are mentioned in verse 3 and also in verses 4-6.

THE VARIETY OF GIFTS (12:4-7)

The Apostle now turns to the gifts of the Holy Spirit. He shows that 12:4 while there is a variety of gifts in the Church, there is a basic, threefold unity, involving the three Persons of the Godhead.

First of all, there are diversities of gifts, but the same Spirit. The Corinthians were acting as if there was only one gift—tongues. Paul says "No, your unity is not found in the possession of one common gift, but rather in possession of the Holy Spirit Who is the Source of all the gifts."

Next the Apostle points out that there are many different minis- 12:5 tries or services in the Church. We don't all have the same work. But what we have in common is that whatever we do is done for the Lord, and with a view to serving others (not self).

Then again, though there are different operations as far as spiritual 12:6 gifts are concerned, it is the same God who empowers each believer. If one gift seems more successful or spectacular or powerful than another, it is not because of any superiority in the person possessing it. It is God who supplies the power.

The Holy Spirit manifests Himself in the life of every believer by 12:7 imparting some gift. There is no believer who does not have a gift, no member of the Body who does not have a function to perform.

And the gifts are given for the benefit of the entire body. They are 12:8 not given for self-display or even for self-edification but in order to help others. This is a pivotal point in the entire discussion.

SOME OF THE GIFTS NAMED (12:8-11)

That leads quite naturally to a list of some of the gifts of the Spirit.

The *word of wisdom* is the supernatural power to speak with divine

103

insight, whether in solving difficult problems, in defending the faith, in resolving conflicts, in giving practical advice or in pleading one's case before hostile authorities. Stephen so demonstrated the word of wisdom that his adversaries "were not able to resist the wisdom and the spirit by which he spoke" (Acts 6:10).

The *word of knowledge* is the power to communicate information that has been divinely revealed. This is illustrated in Paul's use of such expressions as "Behold, I show you a mystery" (1 Cor. 15:51) and "For this we say unto you by the word of the Lord" (1 Thess. 4:15). In that primary sense of conveying new truth, the word of knowledge has ceased, because the Christian faith has been once for all delivered unto the saints (Jude 3). The body of Christian doctrine is complete. In a secondary sense, however, the word of knowledge may still be with us. There is still a mysterious communication of divine knowledge to those who live in close fellowship with the Lord (see Psalm 25:14). The sharing of that knowledge with others is the word of knowledge.

12:9 The gift of *faith* is the divine ability to remove mountains of difficulty in pursuing the will of God (13:2) and to do great exploits for God in response to some command or promise of God as found in His Word or as communicated privately. George Muller is a classic example of a man with the gift of faith. Without ever making his needs known to anyone but God, he cared for 10,000 orphans over a period of sixty years.

The gifts of *healings* have to do with the miraculous power to heal diseases.

12:10 *Workings of miracles* could include casting out demons, changing matter from one form to another, raising the dead, and exercising power over the elements. Philip worked miracles in Samaria, and thereby gained a hearing for the Gospel (Acts 8:6, 7).

The gift of *prophecy,* in its primary New Testament sense, signified that a person received direct revelations from God and transmitted them to others. Sometimes the prophets predicted future events (Acts 11:27, 28; 21:11); more often they simply told forth the mind of God. Like the apostles, they were concerned with the foundation of the Church (Eph. 2:20). They themselves were not the foundation, but they laid the foundation in what they taught concerning the Lord Jesus. Once the foundation was laid, the need for the prophets ceased. Their ministry is preserved for us in the pages of the New

Testament. Since the Bible is complete, we reject any so-called prophet who claims to have additional truth from God.

In a weaker sense, we use the word "prophet" to describe any preacher who declares the Word of God authoritatively, incisively and effectively. Prophecy can also include the ascription of praise to God (Luke 1:67, 68) and the encouragement and strengthening of His people (Acts 15:32).

Discerning of spirits describes the power to detect whether a prophet or other person is speaking by the Holy Spirit or by Satan. A person with this gift has special ability to discern if a man is an imposter and an opportunist, for instance. Thus Peter was able to expose Simon as one who was in the gall of bitterness and in the bond of iniquity (Acts 8:20-23).

The gift of *tongues,* as has been mentioned, is the ability to speak a foreign language without ever having learned it. Tongues were given for a sign, especially to Israel.

The *interpretation of tongues* is the miraculous power to understand a language which the person has never known before and to convey the message in the local language.

It is interesting and perhaps significant that this list of gifts begins with those that are connected primarily with the intellect and closes with those dealing primarily with the emotions. The Corinthians had reversed this in their thinking. They exalted the gift of tongues above the other gifts. They somehow thought that the more a man had of the Holy Spirit, the more he was carried off by a power beyond himself. "They confused power and spirituality" (Wm. Kelly).

"The order that Paul gives is the exact reverse of the estimate of the Corinthians. They believed that when reason and consciousness were least active, one was truly under the power of the Spirit. Paul indicates that the highest spiritual gifts were exercised in connection with the exercise of the reason and the intelligence" (Erdman).

All the gifts mentioned in verses 8-10 are produced and controlled **12:11** by the same Holy Spirit. Here again we see that He does not give the same gift to everyone. He distributes to each one individually as He pleases. This is another important point—the Spirit sovereignly apportions the gifts. If we really grasp this, it will eliminate pride on the one hand, because we don't have anything that we didn't receive. And it will eliminate discontent on the other hand, because Infinite Wisdom and Love decided what gift we should have, and His choice is perfect. It is wrong for everyone to desire the same gift. If everyone played the same instrument, you could never have a symphony orchestra. And if a body consisted only of tongue, it would be a monstrosity.

AN ILLUSTRATION (12:12-31)

12:12 The human body is an illustration of unity and diversity. It is one body, yet has many members. Although all the members are different and perform different functions, yet they all combine to make one functioning unit—the body.

"So also is Christ." More accurately this should be translated, "So also is *the* Christ." "The Christ" here refers not only to the glorified Lord Jesus Christ in heaven, but to the Head in heaven and to His members here upon earth. All believers are members of the body of Christ. Just as the human body is a vehicle by which a person expresses himself to others, so the body of Christ is the vehicle on earth by which He chooses to make Himself known to the world. It is an evidence of wonderful grace that the Lord would ever allow the expression "the Christ" to be used to include those of us who are members of His body.

12:13 Paul goes on to explain how we became members of the body of Christ. By (or in) one Spirit, we were all baptized into one body. The literal translation here is *"in* one Spirit." This may mean that the Spirit is the element in which we were baptized, just as water is the element in which we are immersed in believer's baptism. Or it may mean that the Spirit is the Agent who does the baptizing, thus *"by* one Spirit." This is the more probable and understandable meaning.

The baptism of the Holy Spirit took place on the Day of Pentecost. The Church was born at that time. We partake of the benefits of that baptism when we are born again. We become members of the body of Christ.

Several important points should be noted here: First, the baptism of the Holy Spirit is that divine operation which places believers in the body of Christ. It is not the same as water baptism. This is clear from Matthew 3:11; John 1:33; Acts 1:5. It is not a work of grace subsequent to salvation whereby believers become more spiritual. All the Corinthians had been baptized in the Spirit, yet Paul rebukes them for being carnal, not spiritual (3:1). . . . It is not true that speaking in tongues is the invariable sign of being baptized by the Spirit. All the Corinthians had been baptized, but not all spoke in tongues (12:30). We do not deny that there are crisis experiences of the Holy Spirit when a believer surrenders himself to the Spirit's control and is then empowered from on high. But such an experience is not the same as the baptism of the Spirit, and should not be confused with it.

The verse goes on to say that all believers have been made "to drink into one Spirit." This means that they partake of the Spirit of God in the sense that they receive Him as an indwelling Person and receive the benefits of His ministry in their lives.

Without a variety of members you could not have a human body. **12:14** There must be many members, each one different from the others, working in obedience to the head and in cooperation with the others.

When we see that diversity is essential to a normal, healthy body, it **12:15** will save us from two dangers—from belittling ourselves (vv. 15-20) and from belittling others (vv. 21-25). It would be absurd for the foot to feel unimportant because it can't do the work of a hand. After all, the foot can stand, walk, run, climb, dance—and kick, as well as a host of other things.

The ear shouldn't try to become a dropout because it is not an eye. **12:16** We take our ears for granted till deafness overtakes us. Then we realize what a tremendously useful function they perform.

If the whole body were an eye, you would have a deaf oddity fit **12:17** only for a circus sideshow. Or if the body had only ears, it wouldn't have a nose to detect when the gas was escaping and soon wouldn't even be able to hear because it would be unconscious or dead.

You get the point that Paul is driving at, don't you? If the body were all tongue, it would be a freak, and a monstrosity. And yet the Corinthians were so overemphasizing the gift of tongues that they were, in effect, creating a local fellowship that would be all tongue. It could talk, but that's all it could do.

God hasn't been guilty of such folly. In His matchless wisdom, He **12:18** has arranged the different members in the body as it has pleased Him. We should give Him credit for knowing what He is doing. We should be profoundly grateful for whatever gift He has given us and joyfully use it for His glory and for the edification of others. To be envious of someone else's gift is sin. It is rebellion against God's perfect plan for our lives.

It is impossible to think of a body with only one member. So the **12:19**

Corinthians should remember that if they all had the gift of tongues, then they would not have a functioning body. Other gifts, though less spectacular and less sensational, are nonetheless necessary.

12:20 As God has ordained, there are many members, yet one body. These facts are obvious to us in connection with the human body, and they should be equally obvious to us in connection with our service in the church.

When you are ready, complete Exam 4 by answering questions 11-20 on pages 27-29. (You should have already answered questions 1-10 as part of your study of Lesson 7.)

The Proper Exercise of Gift (12:21—13:13)

OUTLINE

XI. The gifts of the Spirit and their use in the Church (chapters 12-14) (cont'd).

    G. The unity and diversity of the Spirit's work illustrated by the human body (12:12-31) (cont'd).

        4. The folly of a spirit of independence among members (vv. 21-31).

            a. All the members need each other (v. 21).

            b. The feeble members are often more necessary (v. 22).

            c. Members that seem to be uncomely or less honorable deserve special care (v. 23).

            d. God has formed the body by mingling comely and uncomely members (v. 24).

            e. He did this so that there would be harmonious cooperation and mutual care (v. 25).

            f. What affects one member affects all (v. 26).

            g. Christians form the body of Christ, and individually they are members (v. 27).

            h. God has set a variety of gifts in the church (v. 28).

            i. However, no one gift was given to everyone (vv. 29, 30).

            j. We should desire the gifts that are most useful (v. 31).

H. The more excellent way in which gifts should be exercised—namely, in love (Chapter 13).
   1. The uselessness of gifts unless they are lovingly exercised for the benefit of others (vv. 1-3).
   2. The qualities that will characterize those who exercise their gifts in love (vv. 4-7).
   3. The permanence of love contrasted with the temporary character of gifts (vv. 8-12).
   4. The superiority of love to the virtues of faith and hope (v. 13).

In our last lesson we were studying Paul's graphic illustration drawn from the unity and diversity of the human body. The illustration is continued here.

EACH MEMBER IS IMPORTANT (12:21-27)

12:21 Just as it is folly for one person to envy another's gift, so it is equally foolish for anyone to depreciate another's gift or feel that he doesn't need the others. The eye cannot say to the hand, "I have no need of you," or again the head to the feet, "I have no need of you." The eye can see things to be done, but it can't do them. It depends on the hand for that. Again, the head might know that it is necessary to go to a certain place, but it depends upon the feet to take it there.

12:22 Some members of the body seem to be more feeble than others. The kidneys, for instance, don't seem to be as strong as the arms. But the kidneys are indispensable whereas the arms are not. We can live without arms and legs, or even without a tongue, but we cannot live without heart, lungs, liver or brain. Yet these vital organs never put themselves on public display. They just carry on their functions unostentatiously.

12:23 Some members of the body are attractive while others are not so elegant. We compensate by putting clothes over those that are not so beautiful. Thus there is a certain mutual care among the members, minimizing the differences.

12:24 Those parts of the body that are attractive don't need extra attention. But God has combined all the differing members of the body into an organic structure. Some members are comely, some homely. Some do well in public, some not so well. Yet God has given us the instinct to appreciate all the members, to realize that they are all interdependent, and to counterbalance the deficiencies of those that are not so handsome.

The mutual care of the members prevents division or schism **12:25** (pronounced siz-m) in the body. One gives to another what is needed, and receives in return the help that only that other member can give. This is the way it must be in the church. Overemphasis on any one gift of the Spirit will result in conflict and schism.

Next we learn that what affects one member affects all. This is a **12:26** well-known fact in the human body. Fever, for instance, is not confined to one part of the body, but affects the whole system. So it is with other types of sickness and pain. Oftentimes an eye doctor can detect brain tumor, kidney disease, or liver infection by looking into the human eye. The reason is that, although all these members are distinct and separate, yet they all form part of the one body, and they are so vitally linked together that what affects one member affects all. Therefore, instead of being discontent with our lot, or, on the other hand, instead of feeling a sense of independence from others, we should have a real sense of solidarity in the body of Christ. Anything that hurts another Christian should cause us the keenest sorrow. Likewise, if we see another Christian honored, we should not feel jealous, but we should rejoice with him.

Paul reminds the Corinthians that they are the body of Christ. This **12:27** cannot mean *the* body of Christ in its totality. Neither can it mean *a* body of Christ, since there is only one body. It can only mean that they collectively formed a microcosm or miniature of the body of Christ.

Individually each one is a member of that great cooperative society. As such he should fulfill his function without any feeling of pride, independence, envy or worthlessness.

ANOTHER LIST OF GIFTS (12:28-31)

The Apostle now gives us another list of gifts. None of these lists is **12:28** to be considered as complete. "God hath set some in the church, first apostles." The word "some" indicates that not all are apostles. The Twelve were men who had been commissioned by the Lord as His messengers. They were with Him during His earthly ministry (Acts 1:21, 22) and, with the exception of Judas, saw Him after His resurrection (Acts 1:2, 3, 22). But others beside the Twelve were apostles. The most notable was Paul. There were also Barnabas (Acts 14:4, 14); James, the Lord's brother (Gal. 1:19); Silas and Timothy (1 Th. 1:1; 2:6). Together with the New Testament prophets, the apostles laid the doctrinal foundation of the Church in what they taught about the Lord Jesus Christ (Eph. 2:20). In the strict meaning of the word, we no longer have apostles. In a wider sense, we still have messengers and church-planters sent forth by the Lord. By calling them missionaries instead of apostles, we avoid creating the impression that they have the extraordinary authority and power of the early apostles.

Next are the prophets. We have already mentioned that prophets were spokesmen of God, men who uttered the very Word of God in the day before it was given in complete written form. Teachers are those who can take the Word of God and explain it to the people in an understandable way. Miracles might refer to raising the dead, casting out demons, etc. Healings, of course, would have to do with the instantaneous cure of bodily diseases, as mentioned previously. Helps are commonly associated with the work of deacons, those entrusted with the material affairs of the church. Governments, on the other hand, are usually applied to elders or bishops. These are the men who have the godly, spiritual care of the local church. Last is the gift of tongues. We believe that there is a significance in the order. Paul mentions apostles first and tongues last. The Corinthians were putting tongues first and disparaging the Apostle.

12:29
12:30 When the Apostle asks if every believer has the same gift— whether apostle, prophet, teacher, miracles, healings, helps, governments, tongues, interpretations of tongues—he expects and requires a "No" answer. Therefore any suggestion, expressed or implied, that everyone should have the gift of tongues is contrary to the Word of God and is foreign to the whole concept of the body with its many different members.

If, as stated here, not everyone has the gift of tongues, then it is wrong to teach that tongues are the sign of the baptism of the Spirit. For in that case, not everyone could expect the baptism. But the truth is that every believer has already been baptized by the Spirit (v. 13).

12:31 When Paul says "Desire earnestly the greater gifts" (ASV), he is speaking to the Corinthians as a local church, not as individuals. He is saying that as an assembly they should desire to have in their midst a good selection of gifts that edify. The greater gifts are those that are more useful rather than those that are more spectacular. All gifts are given by the Holy Spirit and none should be despised. Yet the fact is that some are of greater benefit to the body than others. These are the ones that every local fellowship should ask the Lord to raise up in the assembly.

"And now I will show you the best way of all" (NEB). With these words Paul introduces the Love Chapter (13). What he is saying is that the mere possession of gifts is not as important as the exercise of these gifts in love. Love thinks of others, not of self. It is wonderful to see a man who is unusually gifted by the Holy Spirit, but it is still more wonderful when that man uses that gift to build up others in the faith rather than to attract attention to himself.

GIFT MUST BE EXERCISED IN LOVE (13:1-13)

People have a tendency to divorce this chapter from its context. They think of it as a parenthesis, designed to relieve the tension over tongues in Chapters 12 and 14. But that is not the case. It is a vital and continuing part of Paul's argument.

The abuse of tongues had apparently caused strife in the assembly. Using their gifts for self-display, self-edification and self-gratification, the "charismatics" were not acting in love. They received satisfaction out of speaking publicly in a language they had never learned, but it was a real hardship on others to have to sit and listen to something they did not understand. Paul insists that all gifts must be exercised in a spirit of love. The aim of love is to help others and not to please self.

And perhaps the "non-charismatics" had overreacted in acts of unlove. They might even have gone so far as to say that all tongues are of the devil. Their Greek tongues might have been worse than "the charismatic" tongues. Their lovelessness might have been worse than the abuse of tongues itself.

So Paul wisely reminds them all that love is needed on both sides of the issue. If they would act in love toward one another, the problem would be largely solved. It is not a problem that calls for excommunication or for division; it calls for love.

1. The Need for Love (13:1-3)

13:1 Even if a person could speak in all languages, human and angelic, but didn't use this ability for the good of others, it would be no more profitable or pleasant than the clanging, jangling sound of metals crashing against each other. Where the spoken word is not understood, there is no profit. It is just a nerve-racking din contributing nothing to the common good. In order for tongues to be beneficial, they must be interpreted, and even then, what is said must be edifying.

13:2 Likewise one might receive marvelous revelations from God. He might understand the great mysteries of God, tremendous truths hitherto unrevealed but now made known to him. He might receive a great inflow of divine knowledge, supernaturally imparted. He might be given that heroic faith which is able to remove mountains. Yet if these wonderful gifts are used only for his own benefit and not for the edifying of other members of the body of Christ, they are of no value, and the holder is nothing, that is, he is of no help to others.

13:3 If the Apostle gave all his goods to feed the poor, or even gave his body to be burned, these valiant acts would not profit him unless they were done in a spirit of love. If he were merely trying to attract attention to himself and to seek a name for himself, then his display of virtue would be valueless.

2. The Nature of Love (13:4-7)

13:4 Someone has said: "This did not start out to be a treatise on love, but like most literary gems of the New Testament, it was introduced in connection with some local situation." Hodge has pointed out that the Corinthians were impatient, discontented, envious, inflated, selfish, indecorous, unmindful of the feelings and interests of others, suspicious, resentful and censorious.

And so the Apostle now contrasts the characteristics of true love. First of all, love suffers long and is kind. Longsuffering is patient endurance under provocation. Kindness is active goodness, going forth in the interests of others. Love does not envy others; rather it is pleased that others should be honored and exalted. Love does not vaunt itself or is not puffed up. It realizes that whatever it has, it is the gift of God, and that there is nothing in man of which to be proud. Even gifts of the Holy Spirit are sovereignly bestowed by

God and should not make a person proud or haughty, no matter how spectacular the gift might be.

Love does not behave itself unseemly. This means that if a person **13:5** is truly acting in love, he will be courteous and considerate. Love does not selfishly seek its own, but is interested in what will assist others. Love is not easily provoked, but is willing to endure slights and insults. Love thinketh no evil, that is, it does not attribute evil motives to others. It does not suspect their actions. It is guileless.

Love does not rejoice in unrighteousness, but rejoices in the truth. **13:6** There is a certain mean streak in human nature which takes pleasure in that which is unrighteous, especially if an unrighteous act seems to benefit one's self. This is not the spirit of love. Love rejoices with every triumph of the truth.

The expression "beareth all things" may mean that love patiently **13:7** endures all things, or that it hides or conceals the faults of others. The word "beareth" may also be translated "covereth." Love does not needlessly publicize the failures of others, though it must be firm in taking godly discipline when necessary.

"Love believes all things," that is, it tries to put the best possible construction on actions and events. Love hopes all things in the sense that it earnestly desires that all things work out for the best. Love endures all things in the way of persecution or ill treatment.

3. The Permanence of Love (13:8-12)

Having described the qualities that characterize those who exercise **13:8** their gift in love, the Apostle now takes up the permanence of love, as contrasted with the temporary character of gifts. Love never fails. Throughout eternity, love will go on in the sense that we will still love the Lord and love one another. These gifts, on the other hand, are of temporary duration.

". . . if there are gifts of prophecy, they will be done away; if there are tongues, they will cease; if there is knowledge, it will be done away" (NASB).

At this point we should pause to explain that there are two principal interpretations of verses 8 through 13. The traditional view is that the gifts of prophecy, tongues and knowledge will cease when believers enter the eternal state. The other view is that these gifts have already ceased, and that this occurred when the Canon of Scripture was completed. In order to present both views, we will paraphrase verses 8 through 12 under the labels ETERNAL STATE and COMPLETED CANON. First, then, we will look at verse 8.

ETERNAL STATE

Love will never cease. In contrast, the prophecies which exist at the present time will be ended when God's people are home in heaven. While there are tongues today, they will cease in and of themselves when eternity replaces time. While there is the gift of knowledge just now, this will be stopped when we reach the final consummation in glory. (When Paul says "knowledge . . . shall vanish away," he cannot mean that there will be no knowledge in heaven. He must be referring to the gift of knowledge whereby divine truth was supernaturally imparted.)

COMPLETED CANON

Love will never cease. While there are prophecies (at the time Paul was writing), the need for such direct revelations would be terminated when the last book of the New Testament would be completed. Tongues were still in use in Paul's day, but they would cease in and of themselves when the sixty-six books of the Bible were finished, because they would no longer be necessary to confirm the preaching of the apostles and prophets (Heb. 2:3, 4). Knowledge of divine truth was being given by God to the apostles and prophets, but this would also be stopped when the complete body of Christian doctrine was once for all delivered.

13:9 In this life our knowledge is partial at best, and so are our prophecies. There are many things we do not understand in the Bible, and many mysteries in the providence of God.

We, that is, the apostles, know in part (in the sense that we are still receiving inspired knowledge by direct revelation from God), and we prophesy in part (because we can only tell forth the partial revelations that we are receiving.)

13:10 But when that which is perfect is come, that is, when we reach the perfect state in the eternal world, then the gifts of partial knowl-

But when that which is perfect is come, that is, when the Canon is completed through the last book's being added to the New

116

edge and partial prophecy will be ended.

This life may be compared to childhood, when our speech, understanding and thought are very limited and immature. The heavenly state is comparable to full manhood. Then our childish condition will be a thing of the past.

As long as we are on earth, we see things dimly and indistinctly, as if we were looking through cloudy glass or in a blurry mirror. Heaven, by contrast, will be like seeing things face to face, that is, without anything between to obscure the vision. Now our knowledge is partial, but then we shall know as we are known—which means more fully. We will never have perfect knowledge, even in heaven. Only God is omniscient. But our knowledge will be vastly greater than it is now.

Testament, then periodic or piecemeal revelations of divine truth will be stopped, and the telling forth of this truth by prophets in fragments will be ended. There will be no more need for partial revelations since the complete Word of God will be here.

13:11 The sign gifts were connected with the childhood of the Church. The gifts were not childish; they were necessary gifts of the Holy Spirit. But once the full revelation of God was available in the Holy Bible, the miracle gifts were no longer needed and were to be put aside.

The word used for *child* here means a baby without the full power of speech (see Young's Concordance).

13:12 Now (during the apostolic age) we see through a glass darkly. No one of us (apostles) has received God's full revelation. It is being given to us in portions, like parts of a puzzle. When the Canon of Scripture is completed, the obscurity will be removed and we will see the picture in its entirety. Our knowledge, as apostles and prophets, is partial at present. But when the last book has been added to the New Testament, we will know more fully and intimately than ever before.

4. The Superiority of Love (13:13)

13:13 Faith, hope and love are what Kelly calls "the main moral principles characteristic of Christianity." These graces of the Spirit are superior to the gifts of the Spirit, and they are more lasting too. In other words, the *fruit* of the Spirit is more important than the *gifts* of the Spirit.

And love is the greatest of the graces because it is most useful to others. It is not self-centered but others-centered.

Now before leaving this chapter, there are a few observations to be made: First, as mentioned above, the generally accepted interpretation of verses 8 through 12 is that they contrast conditions in this life with those in the eternal state.

But many devout Christians hold to the COMPLETED CANON view, believing that the purpose of the sign gifts was to confirm the preaching of the apostles before the Word of God was given in final written form, and that the need for these miracle gifts passed when the New Testament was completed. While this second view merits serious consideration, it can hardly be proved decisively. Even if we believe that the sign-gifts largely passed away at the end of the Apostolic Era, we cannot say with finality that God could not, if He wished, use these gifts today.

Whichever view we hold, the abiding lesson is that while the gifts of the Spirit are partial and temporary, the fruit of the Spirit is eternal and is more excellent. If we practice love, it will save us from the misuse of gifts and from the strife and divisions that have arisen as a result of their abuse.

When you have mastered this lesson, take the first part of Exam 5 (covering lesson 9), questions 1-10 on pages 31-34.

Prophecy and Tongues (14:1-40)

OUTLINE

XI. The gifts of the Spirit and their use in the Church (chapters 12-14) (cont'd).

  I. Instructions concerning the exercise of gifts in the Church (14:1-40).

    1. The gift of prophecy is preferable to that of tongues because it benefits the hearers (vv. 1-5).

    2. In order to profit the Church a message must be understood (vv. 6-11).

      a. Paul uses himself as an example (v. 6).

      b. The same principle is true with musical instruments (vv. 7, 8).

      c. Every voice and language has meaning (vv. 9-11).

    3. Spiritual gifts should be desired as a means of edifying the church (v. 12).

    4. Tongues only serve this purpose when they are interpreted (v. 13).

    5. Others can join in prayer and thanksgiving only when they understand what is being said (vv. 14-17).

    6. It is better to speak and be understood than to be proficient with foreign languages and not be understood (vv. 18, 19).

    7. We should not act to amuse ourselves as children, but should be mature in our evaluation of the gift of tongues (v. 20).

    8. Tongues are a sign to unbelievers, whereas prophecy is a sign to believers (vv. 21, 22).

9. Tongues without interpretation produces no conviction among unbelievers, whereas prophecy does (vv. 23-25).

10. Rules for the exercise of tongues (vv. 26-28).
   a. The messages must be edifying (v. 26).
   b. No more than three may speak in one meeting, and these must speak in turn—not all together (v. 27).
   c. An interpreter must be present (v. 28).

11. Rules governing the prophetic gift (vv. 29-33).
   a. Only two or three prophets may speak in any one meeting (v. 29).
   b. The listeners are to judge the messages (v. 29).
   c. A speaker must give way to another prophet who has just received a revelation (v. 30).
   d. Prophets should speak one at a time, to teach and to comfort (v. 31).
   e. The prophets must be in control of their own faculties (vv. 32, 33).

12. Rules concerning public ministry for women (vv. 33-36).
   a. Women are to remain silent (vv. 33, 34).
   b. They are not even permitted to ask questions (v. 35).
   c. Objections to this are answered with irony (v. 36).

13. The foregoing instructions are the commandments of the Lord (vv. 37, 38).

14. Prophecy should be preferred as more useful (v. 39).

15. Tongues should not be forbidden (v. 39).

16. All should be done decently and in order (v. 30).

PROPHECY IS PREFERABLE TO TONGUES (14:1-5)

14:1 The connection with the previous chapter is apparent. Christians should follow love, and this will mean that they will always be trying to serve others.

They should also earnestly desire spiritual gifts for their assembly. While it is true that gifts are distributed by the Spirit as He wishes, it is also true that we can ask for gifts that will be of greatest value in the local fellowship.

That is why Paul suggests that the gift of prophecy is eminently desirable. He goes on to explain why prophecy, for instance, is of greater benefit than tongues.

The one who speaks in a tongue without interpretation isn't speak- **14:2** ing for the benefit of the congregation. God understands what he is saying but the people don't because it is a foreign language to them. He might be setting forth marvelous truths, hitherto unknown, but it does no good because it is all unintelligible.

(The King James Version speaks of "unknown tongues" but the word "unknown" should be omitted.)

The man who prophesies, on the other hand, builds people up, **14:3** encourages them and comforts them. The reason for this is that he is speaking in the language of the people; that's what makes the difference.

When Paul says that the prophet builds up, stirs up and binds up, he is not giving a definition. He is simply saying that these results follow when the message is given in a language the people know.

Verse 4 is commonly used to justify the private use of tongues for self-edification. But the fact that the word "church" is found nine times in this chapter (vv. 4, 5, 12, 19, 23, 28, 33, 34, 35) offers rather convincing evidence that Paul is not dealing with a man's devotional life in the privacy of his closet, but with the use of tongues in the local assembly.

The context shows that, far from advocating the use of tongues for self-edification, the Apostle is condemning any use of the gift in the church that does not result in helping others. Love thinks of others and not of self. If the gift of tongues is used in love, it will benefit others and not only onself.

The one who prophesies edifies the church. He is not parading his **14:4** gift for personal advantage, but speaking constructively in a language the audience can understand.

Paul does not despise the gift of tongues; he realizes that it is a gift **14:5** of the Holy Spirit. He could not and would not despise anything that comes from the Spirit. When he says, "I would that ye all spake with tongues," he is renouncing any selfish desire to limit the gift to himself and a favored few. His desire is similar to one expressed by Moses, "Would God that all the Lord's people were prophets, and that the Lord would put his Spirit upon them" (Num. 11:29b). But in saying this, Paul knew that it was not God's will that all believers should have any one gift (see 12:29, 30).

121

He would rather that the Corinthians prophesied, because in so doing they would be building up one another, whereas when they spoke in tongues without interpretation, their listeners would not understand and therefore would not be benefited. Paul preferred edification to display. "What astonishes is far less important for the spiritual mind than what edifies"—Kelly.

The expression "except he interpret" could mean "except the one speaking in tongues interpret" or "except someone interpret." The Revised Standard Version translates it "except one interpret."

A MESSAGE MUST BE UNDERSTOOD (14:6-12)

14:6 Even if Paul himself came to Corinth and spoke in tongues, it would not profit them unless they could understand what he said. They would have to be able to recognize what he was saying as revelation or knowledge, or prophesying or teaching. Commentators agree that revelation and knowledge have to do with inward reception, whereas prophesying and teaching have to do with the giving out of the same. Paul's point in this verse is that in order to profit the church, a message must be understood. He goes on to prove this in the following verses.

14:7 First of all, he uses the illustration of musical instruments. Unless a pipe or a harp gives a distinction in the notes, no one will know what is being piped or harped. The very idea of enjoyable music includes the thought of distinction in notes, a definite rhythm, and a certain amount of clarity.

14:8 The same is true of a trumpet. The call to arms must be clear and distinct, otherwise no one will prepare himself for the battle. If the trumpeter merely stands up and blows one long blast in a monotone, no one will stir.

14:9 So it is with the human tongue. Unless the speech we utter is intelligible, no one will know what is being said. It would be as profitless as speaking into the air. (In verse 9 the word tongue means the human tongue instead of a foreign language.) There is a practical application in all of this, namely, that ministry or teaching should be clear and simple. If it is deep and over the heads of the people, then it will not profit them. It might result in bringing a certain measure of gratification to the speaker, but it will not help the people of God.

In verse 10 Paul passes to another illustration of the truth which he **14:10**
has been setting forth. He speaks of the many different kinds of
voices in the world. Here the subject is not languages, but rather the
differing "voices" of creatures throughout the universe. Perhaps Paul
is thinking of the various calls of birds and the squeals and grunts used
by animals. We know, for instance, that there are certain mating calls,
migratory calls, and feeding calls used by birds. Also there are certain
sounds used by animals to indicate the approach of danger. Paul is
simply stating here that all of these voices have a definite meaning.
Not one of them is without significance. Each one is used to convey
some definite message.

It is true also with human voices. Unless a person speaks with **14:11**
articulate sounds, no one can understand him. He might as well be
repeating meaningless gibberish. Few experiences can be more trying than the attempt to communicate with one who does not understand your language.

In view of this, the Corinthians should mingle their zeal for spiri- **14:12**
tual gifts with the desire to edify the Church. "Make the edification
of the church your aim in this desire to excel" (Moffatt). Notice that
Paul never discourages them in their zeal for spiritual gifts, but seeks
to guide and instruct them so that in the use of these gifts they will
reach the highest goal.

TONGUES MUST BE INTERPRETED (14:13-25)

If a man speaks in a tongue, he should "pray that he may interpret." **14:13**
Or the meaning might be "pray that *someone* may interpret." It is
possible that a man who has the gift of tongues might also have the
gift of interpretation, but that would be the exception rather than the
rule. The analogy of the human body suggests different functions for
different members. So although the translation, "pray that *someone*
may interpret," may not be the usual one for this construction, it
seems the most likely one for this context.

If a man, for instance, prays in a tongue at a meeting of the assem- **14:14**
bly, his spirit prays in the sense that his feelings find utterance
though not in the commonly used language. But his understanding is
unfruitful in the sense that it doesn't benefit anyone else. The audience doesn't know what he is saying. As we will explain in the notes
on 14:19, we take the phrase "my understanding" to mean "the

123

understanding of me by others."

14:15 What is the conclusion, then? It is simply this: Paul will not only pray with the spirit, but he will also pray in such a manner as to be understood. This is what is meant by the expression, "I will pray with the understanding also." It does not mean that he will pray with his own understanding, but rather that he will pray so as to help others to understand. Likewise he will sing with the spirit and sing so as to be understood.

14:16 That this is the correct meaning of the passage is made abundantly clear by verse 16. If Paul gave thanks with his own spirit, but not in such a way as to be understood by others, how could one who did not understand the language he was using say "Amen" at the close?

"He that occupieth the room of the unlearned" means a person who is sitting in the audience and does not know the language that is being used by the speaker. This verse incidentally authorizes the intelligent use of the "Amen" in public gatherings of the church.

14:17 Speaking in a foreign language, one might indeed really be giving thanks to God, but others are not edified if they do not know what is being said.

14:18 The Apostle Paul apparently had the ability to speak more foreign languages than any of them. We know that Paul had learned some languages, but here the reference is undoubtedly to his gift of tongues.

14:19 In spite of this superior language ability, Paul says that he would rather speak five words with his understanding, that is, so as to be understood, than to speak ten thousand words in a foreign language. He was not at all interested in using this gift for self-display. His chief aim was to help the people of God. Therefore he determined that when he spoke he would do so in such a way that others would understand him.

The expression "my understanding" is what is known as the objective genitive. It does not mean what I myself understand, but what others understand when I speak.

In his commentary on 1 Corinthians, Charles Hodge agrees that the context here has to do, not with Paul's own understanding of what he spoke in tongues, but of other people's understanding him.

"That Paul should give thanks to God that he was more abundantly endowed with the gift of tongues, if that gift consisted in the ability to speak in languages which he himself did not understand, and the use of which, on that assumption, could according to his principle benefit neither himself nor others, is not to be believed. Equally clear is it from this verse that to speak with tongues was not to speak in a state of mental unconsciousness. The common doctrine as to the nature of the gift is the only one consistent with this passage. Paul says that although he could speak in foreign languages more than the Corinthians, he would rather speak five words *with his understanding,* i.e., so as to be intelligible, than ten thousand words in an unknown tongue. *In the church,* i.e., in the assembly, that I might teach others also (Katecheo) to instruct orally, Gal. 6:6. This shows what is meant by speaking *with the understanding.* It is speaking in such a way as to convey instruction,"

Paul next exhorts the Corinthians against immaturity in their **14:20** thoughts. As Godet has pointed out, "A child prefers the amusing to the useful, the brilliant to the solid." Paul is saying in verse 20, "Don't take a childish delight in these spectacular gifts which you use for self-display. There is one sense in which you should be childlike, and that is in the matter of malice or evil. But in other matters, you should think with the maturity of men."

In verse 21 the Apostle quotes from the Old Testament to show **14:21** that tongues are a sign to unbelievers rather than to believers. God said that because the children of Israel had rejected His message and had mocked it, He would speak to them through a foreign language (Is. 28:11). The fulfillment of this took place when the Assyrian invaders came into the land of Israel, and the Israelites heard the Assyrian language being spoken in their midst. This was a sign to them of their rejection of God's Word.

The argument of verse 22 is that since God intended tongues as a **14:22** sign to unbelievers, the Corinthians should not insist on using them so freely in gatherings of believers. It would be better if they prophesied, since prophesying was a sign for believers and not for unbelievers.

If the whole church were assembled together and all the Christians **14:23** were speaking with tongues without interpretation, what would strangers coming in think about it all? It would not be a testimony to them; rather they would think that the saints were insane.

There is an apparent contradiction between verse 22 and verses 23-25. In verse 22, we are told that tongues are a sign to unbelievers whereas prophecy is for believers. But in verses 23-25, Paul says that tongues used in the church might only confuse and stumble unbelievers whereas prophecy might help them.

The explanation of the seeming contradiction is this. The unbelievers in verse 22 are those who have rejected the Word of God and closed their hearts to the truth. Tongues are a sign of God's judgment on them, as they were on Israel in the Isaiah passage (v. 21). The unbelievers in verses 23-25 are those who are willing to be taught. They are open to hear the Word of God, as is evidenced by their presence in a Christian assembly. If they hear Christians speaking in foreign languages without interpretation, they will be hindered, not helped.

14:24 If strangers enter a meeting where the Christians are prophesying rather than speaking in tongues, the visitors hear and understand what is being said and they are convicted by all and judged by all. What the Apostle is emphasizing here is that no real conviction of sin is produced unless the listeners understand what is being said. When tongues are being used with no interpretation, then obviously visitors are not helped at all. Those who prophesy would, of course, do it in the language in current use in that area, and as a result listeners would be deeply impressed by what they heard.

14:25 The secrets of a man's heart are made manifest by prophecy. He feels that the speaker is addressing him directly. The Spirit of God works conviction in his soul. Thus, falling down on his face he will worship God and report that God is in the midst of these people.

And so Paul's point in verses 22-25 is that tongues without interpretation produce no conviction among unbelievers, whereas prophecy does.

RULES FOR SPEAKING IN TONGUES (14:26-28)

14:26 Because of the abuses that had entered the church in connection with the gift of tongues, it was necessary for the Spirit of God to set forth certain regulations to control the use of this gift. In verses 26 through 28 we have such controls.

What happened when the early church came together? It appears from verse 26 that the meetings were very informal and free. There was liberty for the Spirit of God to use the various gifts which He had given to the church. One man, for instance, would read a Psalm, and then another would set forth some doctrine or teaching. Another would speak in a foreign tongue. Another would present a revelation which he had received directly from the Lord. Another would interpret the tongue that had already been given. Paul gives tacit approval to this "open meeting" where there was liberty for the Spirit of God to speak through different brothers. But having stated this, he sets forth the first control in the exercise of these gifts. Everything must be done with a view to edifying. Just because a thing is sensational or spectacular does not mean that it has any place in the church. In order to be acceptable, ministry must have the effect of building up the people of God. That is what is meant by edifying.

The second control is that in any one meeting no more than three **14:27** may speak in tongues. "If any man speak in an unknown tongue, let it be by two, or at the most by three." There was to be no such a thing as a meeting where a multitude of people would arise to show their proficiency in foreign languages.

Next we learn that the two or three who were permitted to speak in tongues in any one meeting must do so by course. That means that they must not speak at the same time, but in turn—one after the other. This would avoid the bedlam and disorder of several speaking at once.

The third rule is that there must be an interpreter. "Let one interpret." If a man got up to speak in a foreign language, he must first determine that there was someone present to interpret what he was about to say.

If no interpreter was present, then he must keep silence in the **14:28** church. He could sit there and speak inaudibly to God and to himself in this foreign language, but he was not permitted to do so publicly.

RULES FOR PROPHESYING (14:29-33)

Rules for governing the prophetic gift are set forth in verses 29-33a. **14:29** First of all, the prophets were also to speak two or three, and the others were to judge. No more than three were to take part in any one meeting, and the Christians who listened were to determine whether this was truly a divine utterance or whether the man might be a false prophet.

As we have mentioned previously, a prophet received direct **14:30** communications from the Lord and revealed them to the Church. But it is possible that after giving this revelation, he might go on to preach to the people. So the Apostle lays down the rule that if a prophet is speaking and something is revealed to another prophet sitting in the audience, then the first is required to stop speaking to make way for the one who has received the latest revelation. The reason, as suggested, is that the longer the first man talks, the more apt he is to speak by his own power rather than by inspiration. In continued speech there is always the danger of shifting from God's words to one's own words. "Revelation is superior to anything else" (Kelly).

14:31 The prophets should be given the opportunity to speak one at a time. No one prophet should take all the time. In that way, the greatest benefit would result to the church—all would be able to learn and all would be exhorted or comforted.

14:32 A very important principle is set forth in verse 32. Reading between the lines, we suspect that the Corinthians had the false idea that the more a man was possessed by the Spirit of God, the less self-control he had. They felt that he was carried away in a state of ecstasy and they contended, according to Godet, that the more spirit, the less intelligence or self-consciousness there would be. To them, a man under the control of the Spirit was in a state of passivity, and could not control his speech, the length of time he spoke, or his actions in general. Such an idea is thoroughly refuted by the passage of Scripture before us. The spirit of a prophet is subject to the prophet. That means that he is not carried away without his consent, or against his will. He cannot evade the instructions of this chapter on the pretense that he just couldn't help it. He himself can determine when or how long he should speak.

14:33 "For God is not a God of confusion but of peace" (NASB). In other words, if a meeting is the scene of pandemonium and disorder, then you can be sure that the Spirit of God is not in control.

RULES FOR WOMEN (14:34-36)

14:34 In some modern versions, the latter part of verse 33 is linked with verse 34. For instance, in the American Standard Version, we read "As in all the churches of the saints, let the women keep silence in the churches: for it is not permitted unto them to speak; but let them be in subjection, as also saith the law." The instructions which Paul is giving to the Corinthian saints do not apply to them alone. These are

128

the same instructions that have been addressed to all the churches of the saints. The uniform testimony of the New Testament is that while women have many valuable ministries, it is not given to them to have a public ministry in the church. They are entrusted with the unspeakably important work of the home and of raising a family. But they are not allowed to speak publicly in the assembly. Theirs is to be a place of subjection to the man.

We believe that the expression "as also saith the law" has reference to the woman's being in subjection to the man. This is clearly taught in the Law, which here probably means the Pentateuch primarily. Genesis 3:16, for instance, says ". . . and thy desire shall be to thy husband, and he shall rule over thee."

It is often contended that what Paul is forbidding in this verse is for the women to chatter or gossip while the service is going on. However, such an interpretation is untenable. The word here translated "speak" does not mean to chatter. The same word is used of God in verse 21 of this chapter. It means to speak authoritatively.

Indeed, women are not permitted to ask questions publicly in the **14:35** church. If they would learn anything, they should ask their own husbands at home. It is possible that women might try to evade the previous prohibition against speaking by asking questions. Oftentimes it is possible to teach by the simple act of questioning others. So this verse closes any such loophole or objection.

If it be asked how this applies to an unmarried woman or to a woman who is a widow, the answer is that the Scriptures do not try to take up each individual case, but merely set forth general principles. If a woman does not have a husband, she could ask her father or one of the elders of the church. Actually some translations say, "Let them ask their men-folks at home." The basic rule to be remembered is that it is shameful for a woman to speak in the church.

Apparently, the Apostle Paul realized that his teaching here would **14:36** cause considerable contention. To meet any arguments, he uses irony in verse 36 by asking, *"What? came the word of God out from you? or came it unto you only?"* In other words, if the Corinthians professed to know more about these matters than the Apostle Paul did, he would ask them if they, as a church, produced the Word of God, or if they were the only ones who had received it. By their attitude they seemed to set themselves up as an official authority on these matters. But the facts are that no church originated the Word of God, and no church has exclusive rights to it.

THESE RULES ARE FROM GOD (14:37-38)

14:37 In connection with all the foregoing instructions, the Apostle here emphasizes that they are not his own ideas or interpretations, but that they are the commandments of the Lord, and that any man who is a prophet of the Lord or who is truly spiritual will acknowledge that that is the case. This verse is a sufficient answer to those who insist that some of Paul's teachings, especially those concerning women, reflected his own prejudices. These matters are not Paul's private view; they are the commandments of the Lord.

14:38 Of course, some would not be willing to accept them as such, and so the Apostle adds that "if a man be ignorant, let him be ignorant." In other words, if a man refuses to acknowledge the inspiration of these writings and to bow to them obediently, then there is no alternative but for him to continue in his ignorance.

14:39 To sum up the preceding instructions on the exercise of gifts, Paul now tells the Corinthians to desire earnestly to prophesy, but not to forbid men to speak with tongues. This verse shows the relative importance which he placed on these two gifts—one they were to covet earnestly, while the other they were to accept. Prophecy was more valuable than tongues because sinners were convicted through it and saints edified. Tongues without interpretation served no other purpose than to speak to God and to one's self, and to display one's own proficiency with a foreign language, a proficiency that had been given to them by God.

14:40 Paul's final word of admonition is that all things must be done decently and in order. It is interesting that this control should be placed in this chapter. Down through the years, those who have professed to have the ability to speak in tongues have not been noted for the orderliness of their meetings. Rather, many of their meetings have been scenes of uncontrolled emotion and general confusion.

To summarize, then, the Apostle Paul sets forth the following controls for the use of tongues in the local church:

1. We must not forbid the use of tongues (v. 39.).
2. If a man speaks in a tongue, there must be an interpreter (vv. 27c, 28).

3. Not more than three may speak in tongues in any one meeting (v. 27a).
4. They must speak one at a time (v. 27b).
5. What they say must be edifying (v. 26b).
6. The women must be silent (v. 34).
7. Everything must be done decently and in order (v. 40).

These are the abiding controls which apply to the church in our day.

When you are ready, complete Exam 5 by answering questions 11-20 on pages 34-35. (You should have already answered questions 1-10 as part of your study of Lesson 9.)

The Resurrection (15:1-58)

OUTLINE

XII. Paul's answer to those who denied the resurrection (15:1-58).
  A. The resurrection of Christ an established fact of the gospel (vv. 1-11).
    1. The gospel of the resurrection defined (vv. 1-4).
    2. Eye-witnesses of the resurrection (vv. 5-7).
    3. Paul's apostleship based on the resurrection (vv. 8-10).
    4. Unanimous testimony of the apostles (v. 11).
  B. Consequences of the denial of bodily resurrection (vv. 12-19).
    1. It would mean that Christ has not risen (vv. 12, 13).
    2. The apostle's preaching would be vain (v. 14).
    3. One's faith would be vain (v. 14).
    4. The apostles would be deceivers (v. 15).
    5. There would be no salvation from sin (vv. 16, 17).
    6. Those who died in faith would have perished (v. 18).
    7. Living believer would be the most pitiable of men (v. 19).
  C. Results of the resurrection of Christ (vv. 20-28).
    1. The guarantee of the resurrection of those who have died in Christ (vv. 20-22).
    2. The groups involved in the resurrection (vv. 23-28).
      a. Christ, the firstfruits (v. 23).
      b. They that are Christ's at His coming (v. 23).
      c. The end (the resurrection of unbelievers) when all enemies are put under His feet, and Christ's mediatorial work is completed (vv. 24-28).

D. The folly of martyrdom or of suffering for Christ if there is no resurrection (vv. 29-34).
   1. Baptism to fill the ranks of the martyrs would be senseless (v. 29).
   2. The Apostle's sufferings as a Christian would be useless (vv. 30-32).
   3. It would be wiser to live in comfort and pleasure (v. 32).
   4. False teachings about the resurrection affect one's morals, and should not be tolerated (vv. 33, 34).
E. The mode of the resurrection (vv. 35-49).
   1. The resurrection body will have certain features in common with the natural body, but it will be in a glorified form. This is illustrated by the difference between: (vv. 35-41).
      a. Seed and the plant it produces (vv. 35-38).
      b. Human flesh and the flesh of other creatures (v. 39).
      c. Earthly bodies and heavenly bodies (v. 40).
      d. The glory of the sun, of the moon, and of the stars (v. 41).
   2. The believer's body will be: (vv. 42-49).
      a. Incorruptible (v. 42).
      b. Glorious (v. 43).
      c. Powerful (v. 43).
      d. A spiritual body (v. 44).
      e. Like Christ's body (vv. 45-49).
F. The change of living saints at the Lord's return (vv. 50-57).
   1. The dead will be raised and the living will be changed (vv. 50-53).
   2. This will be the victory of all believers over death (vv. 54-57).
G. Final exhortation to stedfastness in view of sure reward at the Lord's coming (v. 58).

In this chapter the Apostle Paul takes up an entirely different subject, that is, the resurrection. Some teachers had entered the church at Corinth, denying the possibility of bodily resurrection. They did not deny the fact of life after death, but probably suggested that we would simply be spirit beings and not have literal bodies. The Apostle here gives his classic answer to these denials.

THE FACT OF THE RESURRECTION (15:1-4)

The Apostle reminds them of the good news which he had preached 15:1
to them, which they had received, and in which they now stood. This
was not a new doctrine for the Corinthians, but it was necessary that
they should be reminded of it at this critical time. It was this gospel 15:2
by which the Corinthians had been saved. Then Paul adds the words
"if ye keep in memory what I preached unto you, unless ye have
believed in vain." The expression "keep in memory" is better translated "hold fast." It was by the gospel of the resurrection that they
had been saved—unless of course, there was no such a thing as
resurrection, in which case they could not have been saved at all. The
"if" in this passage does not express any doubt as to their salvation,
nor does it teach that they were saved by holding fast. Rather, Paul is
simply stating that if there is no such a thing as resurrection, then
they weren't saved at all. In other words, those who denied bodily
resurrection were directing a frontal attack on the whole truth of the
gospel. To Paul, the resurrection was fundamental. Without it there
was no Christianity. Thus this verse is a challenge to the Corinthians
to hold fast the gospel which they had received in the face of the
attacks which were currently being made against it.

The Apostle had delivered to the Corinthians the message which 15:3
he had received by divine revelation. The first cardinal doctrine of
that message was that Christ died for our sins according to the Scriptures. This emphasizes the substitutionary character of the death of
Christ. He did not die for His own sins, or as a martyr; He died for
our sins. He died to pay the penalty that our sins deserved. This was
all according to the Scriptures. The Scriptures here, of course, refer
to the Old Testament Scriptures, since the New Testament was not
yet in written form. Did the Old Testament Scriptures actually pre-
dict that Christ would die for the sins of the people? The answer is an
emphatic yes. Isaiah 53, verses 5 and 6, are sufficient proof of this.

The burial of Christ was prophesied in Isaiah 53:9, and His resur- 15:4
rection in Psalm 16:9, 10. It is important to notice how Paul emphasizes the testimony of the Scriptures. This should ever be the test in
all matters relating to our faith. "What saith the Scriptures?"

In verses 5 through 7, we have a list of those who were eye- 15:5
witnesses of the resurrection. First of all, the Lord appeared to
Cephas, that is, to Peter. This is very touching indeed. The same

faithless disciple who had denied his Lord three times is graciously privileged to have a private appearance of that same Lord in resurrection. Truly, how great is the grace of the Lord Jesus Christ! Then the Lord also appeared to the twelve. This, of course, refers to the twelve disciples. Actually the twelve were not all together at this time, but the expression "the twelve" was used to denote the body of disciples, even though not complete at any one particular moment. It should be stated that not all the appearances which are recorded in the Gospels are mentioned in this list. The Spirit of God selects those resurrection appearances of Christ which He feels to be most pertinent for His use. It should be further noticed that none of the Lord's

15:6 appearances to women are listed here. The Lord's appearance to about five hundred brethren is commonly believed to have taken place in Galilee. At the time Paul wrote, most of these brethren were still living, although some had gone home to be with the Lord. In other words, should anyone wish to contest the truthfulness of what Paul was saying the witnesses were still alive and could be questioned.

15:7 There is no way of knowing for sure just which James is referred to in verse 7, although most commentators assume him to be the Lord's brother. Verse 7 also tells us that the Lord also appeared to all the apostles.

15:8 Paul next speaks of his own personal acquaintance with the risen Christ. This took place, of course, on the road to Damascus, when the Apostle Paul saw a great light from heaven and met the glorified Christ face to face. The expression "one born out of due time" means an abortion or an untimely birth. Vine explains it as meaning that, in point of time, Paul speaks of himself as inferior to the rest of the apostles, just as an immature birth comes short of a mature one. He uses it as a term of self-reproach in view of his past life as a persecutor of the Church.

15:9 As the Apostle thinks of the privilege he had of meeting the Savior face to face, he is filled with a spirit of unworthiness. He thinks of how he persecuted the Church of God and how, in spite of that, the Lord called him to be an apostle. Therefore he bows himself in the dust as the least of the apostles, and not worthy to be called an

15:10 apostle. He hastens to acknowledge that whatever he now is, he is by the grace of God. And he did not accept this grace as a matter of fact. Rather it put him under the deepest obligation, and he labored

136

tirelessly to serve the Christ who saved him. Yet in a very real sense it was not Paul himself, but the grace of God which was working in him.

Now Paul joins himself with the other apostles and states that no 15:11 matter which of them it was who preached, they were all united in their testimony as to the gospel, and particularly as to the resurrection of Christ.

THE IMPORTANCE OF THE RESURRECTION (15:12-19)

In verses 12 through 19, Paul lists the consequences of the denial of 15:12 bodily resurrection. First of all, it would mean that Christ Himself has not risen. Paul's logic here is unanswerable. Some were saying that there is no such thing as bodily resurrection. All right, Paul says, if that is the case, then Christ has not risen. Are you Corinthians willing to admit this? Of course they were not. In order to prove the possibility of any fact, all you have to do is to demonstrate that it has already taken place once. To prove the fact of bodily resurrection, Paul is willing to base his case upon the simple fact that Christ has already risen from the dead. If there is no resurrection of the dead, 15:13 then obviously Christ has not been raised. But such a conclusion would involve the Corinthians in hopeless gloom and despair.

If Christ had not been raised, then the preaching of the Apostles 15:14 was vain, i.e., empty or having no substance. Why was it vain? First of all, because the Lord Jesus had promised that He would rise from the dead on the third day. If He did not rise at that time, then He was either an imposter or was mistaken. In either case, He would not be worthy of trust. Secondly, apart from the resurrection of Christ, there could be no salvation. If the Lord Jesus did not rise from among the dead, then there would be no way of knowing that His death had been of any greater value than any other person's death. But in raising Him from the dead, God testified to the fact that He was completely satisfied with the redemptive work of Christ.

Obviously, if the apostolic message was false, then faith would be also vain. There would be no value in trusting a message that was false or empty. It would not simply be a matter that the apostles were 15:15 preaching a false message; actually it would mean that they had been testifying against God. They witnessed of God that He raised Christ up from the dead. If God didn't do this, then the apostles had been bringing false witness against Him.

15:16 If resurrection is an utter impossibility, then there can be no exception to it. On the other hand, if resurrection had taken place once, for instance, in the case of Christ, then it can no longer be

15:17 thought of as an impossibility. If Christ has not been raised, the faith of believers is vain, that is, futile and devoid of power. And there is no forgiveness of sins. Thus to reject the resurrection is to reject the value of the work of Christ.

15:18 As far as those who had died believing in the Lord Jesus, their case would be absolutely hopeless. If Christ did not rise, then their faith was just a worthless thing. The expression "fallen asleep" refers to the bodies of believers. Sleep is never used of the soul in the New Testament. The soul of the believer departs to be with Christ at the time of death, while the body is spoken of as sleeping in the grave.

We should also say a word concerning the term "perished." This word never means annihilation or cessation of being. As Vine has pointed out, it is not loss of *being,* but rather loss of *well-being.* It speaks of ruin as far as the purpose for which a person or thing was created.

15:19 If Christ is not risen, then living believers are in as wretched a condition as those who have died. They, too, have been deceived. They are of all men most pitiable. Paul is here doubtless thinking of the sorrows, sufferings, trials, and persecutions to which Christians are exposed. To undergo such afflictions for a false cause would be pathetic indeed.

THE RESULTS OF THE RESURRECTION (15:20-28)

15:20 The tension is relieved as Paul triumphantly announces the fact of the resurrection of Christ and of the blessed consequences that ensue. Christ *has* been raised from the dead, the firstfruits of them that are asleep. The student should notice that there is a difference in the Scripture between the resurrection *of* the dead and the resurrection *from* the dead. The previous verses have been dealing with the resurrection of the dead. In other words, Paul has been arguing in a general way that the dead do rise. But Christ rose *from* the dead. This means that when He rose, not all the dead rose. In this sense it was a limited resurrection. "All resurrections are a resurrection of the dead, but only that of Christ and of believers is a resurrection from

138

among dead ones"—Vine.

It was by man that death first came into the world. That man, of **15:21** course, was Adam. Through his sin, death came upon all men. God sent His Son into the world as a Man in order to undo the work of the first man and to raise believers to a state of blessedness such as they could never have known in Adam. Thus it was by the man Christ Jesus that there came the resurrection of the dead. Adam and **15:22** Christ are presented as federal heads. This means that Adam and Christ acted for other people. And all who were related to them were affected by their actions. All who are descended from Adam die. So also in Christ shall all be made alive. This verse has sometimes been taken to teach universal salvation. It is argued that the same ones who die in Adam will be made alive in Christ, and that all will eventually be saved. But that is not what the verse says. The key expressions are "in Adam" and "in Christ." All who are "in Adam" die. All who are "in Christ" will be made alive, that is, only believers in the Lord Jesus Christ will be raised from the dead to dwell eternally with Him. The "all" who shall be made alive (v. 22) is defined in the next verse as "they that are Christ's at His coming." It does not include Christ's enemies, for they shall be put under His feet (v. 25), which, as someone has said, is a strange name for heaven.

Next we have the groups or classes involved in the first resurrec- **15:23** tion. First is the resurrection of Christ Himself. He is spoken of here as the firstfruits. The firstfruits were a handful of ripened grain taken from the harvest field before the actual harvest started. They were a pledge, an earnest, a foretaste of what was to follow. The expression does not necessarily mean that Christ was the first one to rise. We have instances of resurrection in the Old Testament, and the cases of Lazarus, the widow's son, and Jairus' daughter in the New Testament. But Christ's resurrection was different from all of these in the fact that whereas they rose to die again, Christ rose to die no more. He rose to live in the power of an endless life.

The second class in the first resurrection is described as "they that are Christ's, at His coming." This includes those who will be raised at the time of the Rapture, and also those believers who will die during the Tribulation and who will be raised at the end of that time of trouble, when Christ comes back to reign. Just as there are stages in the coming of Christ, so there will be stages in the resurrection of His saints. The first resurrection does not include all who have ever died but only those who have died with faith in Christ.

Some teach today that only those Christians who have been faithful to Christ, or who have been overcomers will be raised at this time, but the Scriptures seem very clear in refuting this. All who are Christ's will be raised at His coming.

15:24 The expression "then cometh the end" refers, we believe, to the end of the resurrection. At the close of Christ's millennial reign, when He shall have put down all His enemies, there will be the resurrection of the wicked dead. This is the last resurrection ever to take place. All who have died in unbelief will stand before the Judgment of the Great White Throne to hear their doom.

After the millennium and the destruction of Satan (Revelation 20:7-10), the Lord Jesus will deliver up the kingdom to God the Father. By that time He will have abolished all rule and authority and power. The thought here is that up to this time the Lord Jesus Christ has been reigning *as the Son of Man,* serving as God's Mediator. At the end of the thousand year reign, God's purposes on earth will have been perfectly accomplished. All opposition will have been put down and all enemies destroyed. The reign of Christ *as Son of Man* will then give way to the eternal kingdom in heaven. His reign *as Son of God* in heaven will continue forever.

15:25 Verse 25 emphasizes what has been just said, namely, that Christ's reign will continue until every trace of rebellion and enmity has been
15:26 abolished. Even during Christ's millennial reign people will continue to die, especially those who openly rebel against the Lord. But at the Judgment of the Great White Throne, death and hades will be cast into the Lake of Fire.

15:27 God has decreed that all things shall be put under the feet of the Lord Jesus. Of course, in putting all things under Him, God necessarily excepted Himself. Verse 27 is rather confusing because it is not clear to whom each pronoun is referring. We might paraphrase it as follows: "For God has put all things under Christ's feet. But when God saith, all things are put under Christ, it is obvious that God is excluded, who put all things under Christ."

15:28 "As Christ will never cease to be Man, He will abide throughout eternity bondman, without derogating from that deity which He ever shares as Son equally with the Father and the Holy Spirit"—W. Kelly. "God has made Christ ruler, administrator of all His plans and counsels. All authority and power is put in His hands. There is a time

140

coming when He will render His account of the administration committed to Him. After He has brought everything into subjection, He will hand the kingdom back to the Father. Creation will be brought back to God in a perfect condition. Having accomplished the work of redemption and restoration for which He became man, He will retain the subordinate place that He took in incarnation. If He should cease to be man after having brought to pass all that God purposed and designated, the very link that brings God and man together would be gone"—Selected.

THE IMPLICATIONS OF THE RESURRECTION (15:29-34)

Verse 29 is perhaps one of the most difficult and obscure verses in all 15:29 the Bible. Many explanations have been offered as to its meaning. For instance, it is contended by some that living believers may be baptized for those who have died without having undergone this rite. Such a meaning, of course, is quite foreign to the Scriptures. It is based upon a single verse alone, and must be rejected. Others believe that to be baptized for the dead means to be baptized for the Lord Who died. Certainly it is true that in baptism we do identify ourselves with Christ in His death, burial, and resurrection. Others believe that baptism for the dead means that in baptism we reckon ourselves to have died. This too is a possible meaning, but it does not fit in too well with the context.

The interpretation which seems to us to suit the context best is this. At the time in which Paul wrote, there was fierce persecution against those who took a public stand for Christ. This persecution was especially vicious at the time of their baptism. It often happened that those who publicly proclaimed their faith in Christ in the waters of baptism were martyred shortly thereafter. But did this stop others from being saved and from taking their place in baptism? Not at all. It seemed as though there were always new replacements coming along to fill up the ranks of those who had been martyred. As they stepped into the waters of baptism, in a very real sense, they were being baptized for, or *in the place of,* the dead. The dead here, then, refers to those who died as a result of their bold witness for Christ. Now the Apostle's argument here is that it would be foolish to be thus baptized to fill up the ranks of those who had died if there is no such thing as resurrection from the dead. It would be like sending

141

replacement troops to fill up the ranks of an army that is fighting a lost cause. It would be like fighting on in a hopeless struggle. "If the dead rise not at all, why are they then baptized for the dead?"

15:30 "And why stand we in jeopardy every hour?" The Apostle Paul's life was constantly exposed to danger. Because of his fearlessness in preaching Christ, he made enemies wherever he went. Secret plots were hatched against him in an effort to take his life. He could have avoided all this by abandoning his profession of Christ. In fact, it would have been wise for him to abandon it if there were no such thing as resurrection from the dead.

15:31 Verse 31 is translated in the New American Standard Bible, "I protest, brethren, by the boasting in you, which I have in Christ Jesus our Lord, I die daily." This might be paraphrased, "As surely as I rejoice over you as my children in Christ Jesus, every day of my life I am exposed to death."

15:32 The Apostle now recalls the fierce persecution which he encountered at Ephesus. We do not believe that he was actually thrown into the arena with wild beasts, but rather that he is speaking here of wicked men as wild beasts. Actually, as a Roman citizen, Paul could not have been forced to fight with wild animals. We do not know just to what incident is referred. However, the argument is clear that the Apostle would have been foolish to engage in such dangerous warfare as he had if he were not assured of resurrection from the dead. Indeed it would have been much wiser for him to adopt the philosophy, "If the dead be not raised, let us eat and drink; for tomorrow we die."

We often hear Christians say that if this life were all, then they would still rather be Christians. But Paul disproves such an idea in this verse. If there is no resurrection, then we would be better off to make the most of this life. We should live for food and clothing and pleasure. This would be the only heaven we could look forward to. But since there is a resurrection, we dare not spend our lives for these things of passing interest. We must live for "then" and not for "now."

15:33 The Corinthians should not be deceived on this score. Evil companionships corrupt good manners. The word "communications" is better translated "companionships." Paul is referring to the false teachers who had come into the church at Corinth. The Christians should realize that it is impossible to associate with evil men or evil

142

teachings without being corrupted by them. Evil doctrine inevitably has an effect on one's life. False teachings do not lead to holiness.

The Corinthians should awake to soberness (righteousness), and **15:34** sin not. They should not be deluded by these evil teachings.

"Some have not the knowledge of God: I speak this to your shame." This verse is commonly interpreted to mean that there are still men and women who have never heard the gospel story, and that the Christians should be ashamed of their failure to evangelize the world. However, we believe that the primary meaning of the passage is that there were men in the fellowship at Corinth who did not have the knowledge of God. They were not true believers, but wolves in sheep's clothing, false teachers who had crept in unawares. It was to the shame of the Corinthians that these men were allowed to take their place with the Christians and to teach these wicked doctrines. "The carelessness which allowed ungodly men to enter resulted in the lowering of the whole moral tone of the church, and prepared the way for the intrusion of every form of error"—Selected.

THE MODE OF THE RESURRECTION (15:35-49)

In verses 35 through 49, the Apostle goes into greater detail con- **15:35** cerning the actual mode of the resurrection. He anticipates two questions which would inevitably arise in the minds of those who questioned the fact of bodily resurrection. The first is "How can the dead be raised?" and the second is "With what kind of a body do they come forth?"

The first question is answered in verse 36. The expression "thou **15:36** fool" might have been translated "thou foolish one" or "thou unthinking one." A common illustration from nature is used to illustrate the possibility of resurrection. A seed must fall into the ground and die before the plant can come forth. It is wonderful indeed to think of the mystery of life that is hidden in every tiny seed. We may dissect the seed and study it under the microscope, but the secret of the life principle remains an unfathomable mystery. All we know is that the seed falls into the ground and from that unlikely beginning there springs forth life from the dead.

The second question is taken up now. Paul explains that when you **15:37** sow a seed, you do not sow the plant that will eventually result, but you sow a bare grain, whether of wheat or of some other kind. What do we conclude from this? Is the plant the same as the seed? No, the plant is not the same as the seed; however, there is a very vital connection between the two. Without the seed there would have been no plant. Also, the plant derives its features from the seed. So it is in resurrection. "The resurrection body has identity of kind and continuity of substance with that which is sown, but it is purified from corruption, dishonor, and weakness, and made incorrupt, glorious, powerful, and spiritual. It is the same body, but it is sown in one form and raised in another"—Selected.

15:38   God produces a body according to the seed that was sown, and every seed has its own type of plant resulting therefrom. All the factors which determine the size, color, leaf, and flower of the plant are somehow contained in the seed that is sown.

15:39   To illustrate the fact that the glory of the resurrection body will be different from the glory of our present bodies, the Apostle Paul points out that all flesh is not the same kind. For instance, there is human flesh, animal flesh, the flesh of birds, and the flesh of fishes. These are distinctly different, and yet they are all flesh. There is similarity without exact duplication.

15:40   And just as there is a difference between the glory of heavenly bodies (the stars, etc.,) and the bodies which are associated with this earth, so there is a difference between the body of the believer now
15:41 and the one which he will have after death. Even among the celestial bodies themselves, there is a difference of glory. For instance, the sun is brighter than the moon, and the stars differ among themselves as to their brightness.

Most commentators agree that Paul is still emphasizing that the glory of the resurrection body will be different from the glory of the body which we have on earth at the present time. They do not think that verse 41, for instance, indicates that in heaven there will be differences of glory among believers themselves. However, we tend to agree with Holsten that "the way in which Paul emphasizes the diversities of the heavenly bodies implies the supposition of an analogous difference of glory between the risen." It is clear from other passages of Scripture that we shall not all be alike in heaven. Although all will resemble the Lord Jesus morally, that is, in freedom from sin, it does not follow that we shall all look like the Lord Jesus physically. He will be distinctly recognizable as such throughout all eternity. Likewise we believe that each individual Christian will be a distinct personality recognizable as such. But there will be differences of reward granted at the Judgment Seat of Christ according to one's faithfulness in service. While all will be supremely happy in heaven, some will have greater capacity for enjoying heaven. Just as there will be differences of suffering in hell, according to the sins that a man has committed, so there will be differences of enjoyment in heaven, according to what we have done as believers.

Verses 42 through 49 show the contrast between what the be- **15:42** liever's body is now and what it will be in its eternal state. "It is sown in corruption; it is raised in incorruption." At the present time, our bodies are subject to disease and death. When they are placed in the grave, they decompose and return to dust. But it will not be so with the resurrection body. It will no longer be subject to sickness or decay.

The present body is sown in dishonor. There is nothing very **15:43** majestic or glorious about a dead body. However, this same body will be raised in glory. It will be free from wrinkles, scars, the marks of age, and the traces of sin.

It is sown in weakness; it is raised in power. With the coming of old age, weakness increases until death itself strips a man of all strength whatever. In eternity, the body will not be subject to these sad limitations, but will be possessed of powers that it does not have at the present time. For instance, the Lord Jesus Christ in resurrection was able to enter a room where the doors were locked.

It is sown a natural body; it is raised a spiritual body. Here we must **15:44** be very careful to emphasize that spiritual does not mean non-material. Some people have the idea that in resurrection we will be disembodied spirits. That is not at all the meaning of this passage, nor is it true. We know that the resurrection body of the Lord Jesus was composed of flesh and bones because He said, "A spirit hath not flesh and bones, as ye see me have" (Luke 24:39). The difference between a natural body and a spiritual body is that the former is suited to life here on earth whereas the latter will be suited to life in heaven. The former is usually soul-controlled whereas the latter is spirit-controlled. A spiritual body is one that will be truly the servant of the spirit.

God created man spirit, soul, and body. He always mentions the spirit first, because His intention was that the spirit should be in the place of preeminence or dominance. With the entrance of sin, some-

145

thing very strange happened. God's order seems to have been upset, and the result is that man always says "body, soul, and spirit." He has given the body the place which the spirit should have had. In resurrection it will not be so, but the spirit will be in the place of control which God originally intended.

15:45 "So also it is written, 'The first man Adam became a living soul. The last Adam *became* a life-giving spirit' (NASB). Here again the first Adam is contrasted with the Lord Jesus Christ. God breathed into the former's nostrils the breath of life and he became a living soul (Gen. 2:7). All who are descended from him bear his characteristics. The last Adam, the Savior, became a life-giving Spirit (John 5:21, 26). The difference is that in the first case, Adam was given physical life, whereas in the second case Christ gives eternal life to others. "As the descendants of Adam, we are made like him, living souls inhabiting mortal bodies, and bearing the image of an earthly parent. But as the followers of Christ, we are yet to be clothed with immortal bodies and to bear the image of our heavenly Lord"— Eerdman.

Verse 45 in the New American Standard Bible is preferable to the King James Translation. The latter says that the last Adam was made a quickening spirit. The words "was made" were supplied by the translators. It would be unfortunate if they should suggest to a reader that the Lord Jesus was a created being. He is the eternal God, without beginning of days or end of life.

15:46 The Apostle now sets forth a fundamental law in God's universe, namely, the spiritual is not first, but the natural; then the spiritual. This can be understood in several ways. Adam, the natural man came first on the stage of human history, then Jesus, the spiritual Man. Second, we are born into the world as natural beings; then when we are born again, we become spiritual beings. Finally, we first receive natural bodies, then in resurrection we will receive spiritual bodies.

15:47 *"The first man is of the earth, earthy."* This means that his origin was of the earth and that his characteristics were earthy. He was made of the dust of the ground in the first place, and in his life he seemed in a very real sense to be earth-bound. The King James Version says the
15:48 second man is the Lord from heaven. Of the two men mentioned in verse 45, Jesus was the second. Of course, He existed from all eternity, but as Man, he came after Adam. He came from heaven, and everything he did and said was heavenly and spiritual rather than

146

earthly and soulish.

Several New Testament manuscripts omit the words "the Lord" and read "the second man (is) from heaven." But this does not change the meaning of the verse.

As it is with these two federal heads, so it is with their followers. Those who are born of Adam inherit his characteristics. Also those that are of Christ are a heavenly people. As we have borne the **15:49** characteristics of Adam as to our natural birth, so we shall bear the image of Christ in our resurrection bodies.

THE EFFECT OF THE RESURRECTION (15:50-58)

In verse 50 the Apostle turns to the subject of the transformation **15:50** that will take place in the bodies of believers, both living and dead, at the time of the Lord's return. He prefaces his remarks with the statement that flesh and blood cannot inherit the kingdom of God. By this he means that the present body which we have is not suited to the kingdom of God in its eternal aspect, that is, our heavenly home. It is also true that corruption cannot inherit incorruption. In other words, our present bodies which are subject to disease, decay, and decomposition would not be suited for life in a state where there is no corruption. This raises the problem, then, of how the bodies of living believers can be suited for life in heaven.

The answer is in the form of a mystery. As previously stated, a **15:51** mystery is a truth hitherto unknown, but now revealed by God to the apostles and made known through them to us.

"We shall not all sleep, but we shall all be changed." Not all believers will go through the article of death. Some will be alive when the Lord returns. But whether we have died or are still alive, we shall all be changed. The truth of resurrection itself is not a mystery, since it was mentioned in the Old Testament, but the change of living saints at the Lord's return is something that had never been known before.

The change will take place instantly, *"in the twinkling of an eye, at* **15:52** *the last trump."* The last trump here does not mean the end of the world, or even the last trumpet mentioned in Revelation. Rather, it refers to the trump of God which will sound when Christ comes into the air for His saints. We read of this trump in 1 Thessalonians 4:16. When the trumpet sounds, the dead shall be raised incorruptible, and the living will be changed. What a tremendous moment that will be, when the earth and the sea will yield up the dust of all those who have died trusting in Christ down through the centuries! It is almost impossible for the human mind to take in the magnitude of such an event; yet the humble believer can accept it by faith.

15:53 We believe that verse 53 refers to the two classes of believers at the time of Christ's return. "This corruptible" refers to those whose bodies have returned to the dust. They will put on incorruption. "This mortal," on the other hand, refers to those who are still alive in body but are subject to death. Such bodies will put on immortality.

15:54 When the dead in Christ shall be raised and the living changed with them, then will be brought to pass the saying that is written, "Death is swallowed up in victory" (Isaiah 25:8). "How magnificent! What are death, the grave and decomposition in the presence of such power as this? Talk of being dead four days as a difficulty! Millions that have been mouldering in the dust for thousands of years shall spring up in a moment into life, immortality and eternal glory at the voice of the Blessed One"—C. H. Mackintosh.

15:55 According to the best manuscripts, verse 55 should read, "O death, where is thy victory? O death, where is thy sting?" This is a taunt song which believers will sing as they rise to meet the Lord in the air. It is as if they mock death because its victory has been partial and temporary—partial because not all died and temporary because those who did die are now alive forevermore. They also mock death because, for them it has lost its sting. Death holds no terror for them because they know their sins have been forgiven and they stand before God in all the acceptability of His beloved Son.

15:56 Death would have no sting for anyone if it were not for sin. It is the consciousness of sins unconfessed and unforgiven that makes men afraid to die. If we know our sins are forgiven, we can face death with confidence. If, on the other hand, sin is on the conscience, death is terrible—the beginning of eternal punishment.

The strength of sin is the law. This means that the law condemns the sinner. It pronounces the doom of all who have failed to obey God's holy precepts. It has been well said that if there were no sin, there would be no death. And if there were no law, there would be no condemnation. "The throne of death rests on two bases: sin, which calls for condemnation, and the law which pronounces it. Consequently, it is on these two powers that the work of the Deliverer **15:57** bore"—Godet. Through faith in Him, we have victory over death and the grave. Death is robbed of its sting. It is a known fact that when certain insects sting a person, they leave their sting imbedded in the person's flesh, and being thus robbed of their sting, they die. In a very real sense death stung itself to death at the Cross of Christ and now the King of Terrors is robbed of his terror as far as the believer is concerned.

In view, then, of the certainty of the resurrection and the fact that 15:58 faith in Christ is not in vain, the Apostle Paul exhorts his beloved brethren to be steadfast, unmovable, always abounding in the work of the Lord, knowing that their labor is not in vain in the Lord. The truth of resurrection changes everything. It provides hope and steadfastness, and enable us to go on the face of overwhelmingly difficult circumstances.

When you have mastered this lesson, take the first part of Exam 6 (covering lesson 11), questions 1-10 on pages 37-39.

Lesson 12

In Conclusion (16:1-24)

OUTLINE

XIII. Instructions concerning the collection (16:1-4).
    A. The manner of collecting the funds (vv. 1, 2).
    B. The manner of delivering it to Jerusalem (vv. 3, 4).
XIV. Paul's personal plans (16:5-9).
 XV. Closing exhortations and greetings (16:10-24).
    A. Plea to receive Timothy cordially (vv. 10, 11).
    B. Plan of Apollos to visit Corinthians (v. 12).
    C. Exhortations to steadfastness and love (vv. 13, 14).
    D. Plea to honor the house of Stephanas (vv. 15, 16).
    E. Plea to acknowledge Stephanas, Fortunatus, and Achaicus (vv. 17, 18).
    F. Greetings from the saints in Asia (vv. 19, 20).
    G. Paul's own salutation (vv. 21-24).

The first verses of this chapter concern an offering which was to be taken up by the church in Corinth and sent to needy saints in Jerusalem. The exact cause of their poverty is not known. Some have suggested that it was a result of famine (Acts 11:28-30). Possibly another reason is that those Jews who professed faith in Christ would be ostracized and boycotted by their unbelieving relatives, friends, and fellow countrymen. They would doubtless lose their jobs and in countless other ways be subjected to economic pressures designed to force them to give up their profession of faith in Christ.

CONCERNING THE COLLECTION (16:1-4)

Paul had already given instructions to the churches of Galatia in **16:1**

151

connection with this very matter, and he now instructs the Corinthians to respond in the same manner that the Galatian saints had been exhorted to do.

16:2   Although the instructions given in verse 2 were for a specific collection, yet the principles involved are of abiding value. First of all, the laying by of funds was to be done on the first day of the week. Here we have a very strong indication that the early Christians no longer regarded the Sabbath or seventh day as an obligatory observance. The Lord had risen on the first day of the week, the day of Pentecost was the first day of the week, and the disciples gathered together on the first day of the week to break bread. Now they are to lay by in store on the first day of the week.

The second important principle is that the instructions concerning the collections were for everyone. Rich and poor, bond and free were all to have part in the sacrifice of the giving of their possessions.

Again we learn that this was to be done systematically. On the first day of the week they were to lay by them in store. It was not something that was haphazard, or reserved for special occasions. The gift was to be set aside from other money and devoted to special use as occasion demanded.

Again we see that their giving was to be proportionate. This is indicated by the expression "as God hath prospered him."

"That no collections be made when I come" (NASB). The Apostle Paul did not want this to be a matter of last-minute arrangement. He realized the serious possibility of giving without due preparation of heart or pocketbook.

16:3   Verses 3 and 4 give us very valuable insight into the care that should be taken with funds that are gathered in a Christian assembly. It is noticeable, first of all, that the funds were not to be entrusted to any one person. Even Paul himself was not to be the sole recipient. Secondly, we notice that the arrangements as to who would carry the money were not made arbitrarily by the Apostle Paul. Rather, this decision was left to the local assembly. When they selected the messengers, Paul would send them with letters to Jerusalem. Perhaps the reason for the Apostle's writing the letters was that he would know the saints in Jerusalem better than the Corinthian believers would, and therefore these letters would serve as an introduction for the messengers from the church at Corinth.

16:4   If it was decided that it would be well for the Apostle Paul to go to

Jerusalem also, then the local brethren would accompany him there. It is noticeable that he says "they shall go with me" rather than "I shall go with them." Perhaps this is an allusion to Paul's authority as an apostle. Some commentators suggest that the factor that would determine whether Paul went or not would be the size of the gift, but we would hardly believe that the great Apostle would be guided by such a principle.

PAUL'S PLAN (16:5-9)

The Apostle discusses his personal plans in verses 5-9. You will **16:5** remember that he was in Ephesus when he wrote this letter. From Ephesus he planned to go to Macedonia. (The student should trace this on a map.) Then he hoped to move south to Corinth after he had been in Macedonia. The expression "I do pass through Macedonia" means "my plan is to pass through Macedonia." It is possible that **16:6** Paul would spend the winter with the saints in Corinth and then they would speed him on his way, wherever he would go from there. For **16:7** the present, then, he would not see them enroute to Macedonia, but he did look forward to staying with them later for a while, if the Lord would so permit.

Before leaving for Macedonia, Paul expected to tarry at Ephesus **16:8** until Pentecost. It is from this verse that we learn that the epistle was written from Ephesus, rather than from Philippi (as stated at the end of this letter in the subscript of the Authorized Version). Paul **16:9** realized that there was a golden opportunity for serving Christ at that time at Ephesus. At the same time he realized that there were many adversaries. What an unchanging picture this verse gives us of Christian service. On the one hand, there are the fields white already to harvest: on the other, there is a sleepless foe who seeks to obstruct, divide, and oppose in every conceivable way.

CLOSING EXHORTATIONS AND GREETINGS (16:10-24)

The Apostle adds a word concerning Timothy. If this devoted young **16:10** servant of the Lord came to Corinth, they should receive him without fear. Perhaps this means that Timothy was naturally of a timid disposition, and that they should not do anything to intensify this tendency. Perhaps, on the other hand, it means that he should be able to come to them without any fear of not being accepted as a

153

servant of the Lord. That the latter is probably the proper meaning is indicated by the words, "For he worketh the work of the Lord, as I 16:11 also do." Because of Timothy's faithful service for Christ, no man should despise him. Instead, an earnest effort should be made to set him forward on his journey in peace that he might return to Paul in due time. The Apostle was looking forward to a reunion with Timothy and with the brethren.

16:12 With regard to Apollos, the brother, Paul had urged him to visit Corinth with the brothers. Apollos did not feel that this was God's will for him at this time, but he indicated that he would go to Corinth when he had the opportunity. Verse 12 is valuable to us in showing the loving spirit that prevailed among the servants of the Lord involved. Someone has called it a beautiful picture of "unjealous love and respect." It also shows the liberty that prevailed for each servant of the Lord to be guided by the Lord without dictation from any other source. Even the Apostle Paul himself was not authorized to tell Apollos what to do. In this connection Dr. H. A. Ironside has commented, "I would not like to tear this chapter out of my Bible. It helps me to understand God's way of guiding His servants in their ministry for Him."

16:13 Now Paul delivers some pithy exhortations to the saints. They are to be constantly on guard, to stand fast in the faith, to quit themselves like men and to be strong. Perhaps Paul is thinking again of the danger of false teachers. The saints are to be on guard all the time. They are not to give up an inch of vital territory. They are to behave with true manly courage. Finally, they are to be strong in the 16:14 Lord and in the power of His might. In all that they do, they are to manifest love. This will mean lives of devotion to God and to others. It will mean a giving of themselves.

16:15 Next follows an exhortation concerning the house of Stephanas. These dear Christians were the firstfruits of Achaia, that is, the earliest converts in Achaia. (In Romans 16:5, Epaenetus is spoken of as the firstfruits of Achaia, but the correct translation in the Romans passage should be *Asia* instead of *Achaia*.) Apparently from the time of their conversion, these believers had addicted themselves to the ministry of the saints. "Ministry" here means simply service. Paul is saying that these Christians set themselves to serve the people of God.

The household of Stephanas was mentioned previously in chapter

1, verse 16. There Paul states that he baptized the household. Many have insisted that the household of Stephanus included infants and have sought thereby to justify the baptism of babies. However, it seems rather clear from verse 15 of this chapter that there were no infants in this household, since it is distinctly stated that they addicted themselves to the ministry of the saints. The Apostle exhorts **16:16** the Christians to be in subjection to such, and to everyone who helps in the work and who labors. It seems clear from the general teaching of the New Testament that those who set themselves apart for the service of Christ should be shown the loving respect of all the people of God. If this were done more generally, it would avoid a great deal of faction and jealousy.

The coming of Stephanas and Fortunatus and Achaicus had **16:17** brought joy and cheer to the heart of the Apostle. They had supplied what was lacking on the part of the Corinthians. This may mean that they showed kindness to the Apostle which the Corinthians had neglected to do. Or more probably it means that what the Corinthians were unable to do because of their distance from Paul, these men had accomplished. Thus the Amplified New Testament translates, "They have made up for your absence. . . ." They brought news from **16:18** Corinth to Paul, and conversely they brought back news from the Apostle to their home assembly. Again Paul commends them to the loving respect of the local church.

In the expression, "the churches of Asia," Asia does not mean the **16:19** continent, but rather the province. Ephesus was located in that province.

Aquila and Priscilla were apparently living in Ephesus at this time. At one time previously they had lived in Corinth, and thus were known to the saints there. Aquila was a tentmaker by trade, and had worked with the Apostle Paul in this occupation. The expression *"the church that is in their house"* gives us a view of the simplicity of assembly life at that time. Christians would gather together in their homes for worship, prayer, and fellowship. Then they would go out to preach the gospel at their work, in the market place, in the local prison, and wherever their lot was cast.

All the brethren in the assembly join in sending loving greetings to **16:20** their fellow believers in Corinth. The Apostle enjoins his readers to salute one another with a holy kiss. At that time, the kiss was a common mode of greeting, even among men. A holy kiss means a greeting without sham or impurity. In our sex-obsessed society, where perversion is so prevalent, the widespread use of the kiss as a mode of greeting might present serious temptations and lead to gross moral failures. For that reason, the handshake has largely taken the place of the kiss among Christians in our culture. . . . Ordinarily we should not allow cultural considerations to excuse strict adherence to the words of Scripture. But in a case like this, where literal obedience might lead to sin because of local cultural conditions, we are justified in substituting the handshake for the kiss.

16:21 Paul's usual habit was to dictate his letters to one of his co-workers. However, at the end he would take the pen in his own hand, add a few words in his own writing, and then give his characteristic greeting. That is what he does at this point. He salutes the brethren in his own handwriting.

16:22 The word "Anathema" means cursed. The word "Maran-atha" means "The Lord cometh." The simple meaning of the verse is that those who do not love the Lord Jesus are condemned already but that their doom will be manifest at the coming of the Lord Jesus Christ. In a very real way, a Christian is one who loves the Savior. He loves the Lord Jesus more than anyone or anything in the world. Failure to love God's Son is a crime against God Himself. "St. Paul allows no way of escape to the man who does not love Christ. He leaves no loophole or excuse. A man may lack clear head-knowledge and yet be saved. He may fail in courage, and be overcome by the fear of man, like Peter. He may fall tremendously, like David, and yet rise again. But if a person does not love Christ he is not in the way of life. The curse is yet upon him. He is on the broad road that leadeth to destruction"—Ryle.

16:23 Grace was Paul's favorite theme. He loved to open and end his letters on the exalted note. It is one of the true marks of his authorship.

16:24 Throughout the entire epistle we have listened to the heartbeat of this devoted apostle of Jesus Christ. We have listened to him as he sought to edify, comfort, exhort, and admonish his children in the faith. There was no doubt that he loved them. When they read these closing words, perhaps they would feel ashamed that they had allowed false teachers to come in, questioning Paul's apostleship and turning them away from their original love for him.

When you are ready, complete Exam 6 by answering questions 11-20 on pages 39-42. (You should have already answered questions 1-10 as part of your study of Lesson 11.)

BIBLIOGRAPHY

Barnes, Albert, *Notes on the New Testament*. (Vol. V, 1 Corinthians). London: Blackie & Son, No date.

Christenson, Larry. *The Christian Family*. Minneapolis: Bethany Fellowship, 1970.

Darby, J. N. *Synopsis of the Books of the Bible*. (Vol. IV). New York: Loizeaux Bros., 1942.

Davies, J. M. *The Epistles to the Corinthians*. Bombay: Gospel Literature Service, 1975.

Erdman, Charles R. *The First Epistle of Paul to the Corinthians*. Philadelphia: Westminster Press, 1928.

Godet, F. *Commentary on First Corinthians*. Edinburgh: T & T Clark, No date.

Grant, F. W. *Numerical Bible*. (Acts-2 Cor.). New York: Loizeaux Bros., No date.

Hodge, Charles. *An Exposition on the First Epistle to the Corinthians*. New York: George H. Doran Company, 1857.

Ironside, H. A. *Addresses on the First Epistle to the Corinthians*. New York: Loizeaux Bros., 1955.

Kelly, William. *Notes on the First Epistle to the Corinthians*. London: G. Morrish, 1878.

Meyer, F. B. *Through the Bible Day by Day*. (Vol. 6) Philadelphia: American S. S. Union, 1918.

Pfeiffer, Charles F. and Harrison, Everett F., Editors. *The Wycliffe Bible Commentary*. Chicago: Moody Press, 1962.

Rogers, E. W. *Concerning the Future*. Chicago: Moody Press, 1962.

Ryle, J. C. *Practical Religion*. London: Jas. Clarke & Co., Ltd., 1959.

Ryrie, Charles C. *The Ryrie Study Bible*. Chicago: Moody Press, 1976.

Vine, W. E. *First Corinthians*. London: Oliphants Ltd., 1951.

Vine, W. E. *Expository Dictionary of New Testament Words*. Old Tappan, N. J.: Fleming H. Revell Co., 1966.

Vine, W. E. *The Divine Plan of Missions*. London: Pickering & Inglis, Ltd., No date.

Wuest, Kenneth S. *In These Last Days*. Grand Rapids: Wm. B. Eerdmans Publishing Co., 1954.

Bible Versions Used:

American Standard Version.
Revised Version,
New Translation—J. N. Darby.
Amplified New Testament.
New American Standard Bible.
Revised Standard Version.
Today's English Version.
New English Bible.
New International Version.
The Bible—James Moffatt.
The Holy Bible—Ronald Knox.

In addition to the above, isolated quotations have been made from the writings of A. T. Robertson, H. P. Barker, A. T. Pierson, E. H. Bates, F. B. Hole, Dr. Rendall Harris, A. T. Schofield, C. H. Mackintosh, Wm. Arnot, Ter Steegen, Eric Sauer, Traill, Vance Havner, Henrici, F. G. Patterson and Holsten. It is no longer possible to document these accurately.

NOTES

NOTES

NOTES

NOTES

NOTES

NOTES

NOTES

NOTES

NOTES

NOTES

NOTES

NOTES